saint J. D.

# saint J. D.

by

James Cole and Robert Lee

WORD BOOKS, Publishers
Waco, Texas—London, England

Library of Congress Catalog Card Number
70–85829. Printed and manufactured in the
United States of America.

# CONTENTS

*Dedicated to those who
know J. D. and love him
nonetheless*

In the year of the dove and the hawk, even an amateur bird watcher would be forced to conclude that J. D. Grey is a rare bird. In a real sense he has soared to greater heights than the average man ever dreams of attaining by hook and ladder or satellite.

The centerpiece of Baptist life in New Orleans for over thirty years, he is more colorful than a Mardi Gras parade, more diverse than the Vieux Carré, more dynamic than the great ships riding in the harbor of the city. Although he is void of the trappings of piosity, he is a genuine New Testament saint. St. J. D. would never accept canonization from any name brand denomination, but he would acquiesce to the title if it were offered "prehumorously." Medallions celebrating his twenty-fifth anniversary as pastor of First Baptist Church, New Orleans, have circulated around the world by the thousands as St. J. D. medals.

One of his favorite admonitions to young preachers is, "Your halo is too tight." The only thing about J. D. that resembles a halo is the circling smoke of a panatella. A man without sham or pretense, his orthodoxy is neither dull nor rigid, but flexible and refreshing. Although dueling may be an outlawed, dead sport in the Crescent City, he carries with him the Sword of Truth to fight the battles in the public arena for law and order.

J. D. was not born with a silver shoe in his mouth. He hails from the hills of Kentucky, but his quip draw is faster than any word slinger from the Wild West. His instant humor has dissolved many a tense moment and kept public meetings from developing into Baptist brawls. He could have been a columnist, comedian or clown, a public relations expert, a statesman or diplomat, even a politician defending an unpopular platform. A man of many hats, he has, in fact, been all of these when the occasion demanded a new style. Whatever hat he wears for the moment, his first love is the pulpit in the historic First Baptist Church of New Orleans.

At times his modesty shows. When this book was first mentioned, he characteristically thought it a joke, but consented only if "warts and all" were part of the finished painting.

What is St. J. D. really like? In his days as a pledge of ATO at Union University, Jackson, Tennessee, he was required to memorize Kipling's poem, "If." In the intervening years, this poem has become an essential part of his personal philosophy.

# IF

*If you can keep your head when all about you*
*Are losing theirs and blaming it on you,*
*If you can trust yourself when all men doubt you,*
*But make allowance for their doubting too;*
*If you can wait and not be tired by waiting,*
*Or being lied about, don't deal in lies,*
*Or being hated, don't give way to hating,*
*And yet don't look too good, nor talk too wise:*

*If you can dream—and not make dreams your master;*
*If you can think—and not make thoughts your aim;*
*If you can meet with Triumph and Disaster*
*And treat those two impostors just the same;*
*If you can bear to hear the truth you've spoken*
*Twisted by knaves to make a trap for fools,*
*Or watch the things you gave your life to, broken,*
*And stoop and build 'em up with worn-out tools.*

*If you can make one heap of all your winnings*
*And risk it on one turn of pitch-and-toss,*
*And lose, and start again at your beginnings*
*And never breathe a word about your loss;*
*If you can force your heart and nerve and sinew*
*To serve your turn long after they are gone,*
*And so hold on when there is nothing in you*
*Except the Will which says to them: "Hold on!"*

*If you can talk with crowds and keep your virtue,*
*Or walk with Kings—nor lose the common touch,*
*If neither foes nor loving friends can hurt you,*
*If all men count with you, but none too much;*
*If you can fill the unforgiving minute*
*With sixty seconds' worth of distance run,*
*Yours is the Earth and everything that's in it,*
*And—which is more—you'll be a Man, my son!*

Rudyard Kipling

## Merci Beaucoup

The authors are indebted to many people in the preparation of the manuscript. Acknowledging that debt in whatever language is needful.

Appreciation is felt for the following because of their assistance: Jinks Mahnker, Evelyn Patterson, Thalia Ellis, Velma Fousse, Louise Cobb, Dorothy Bankston, Davis L. Cooper, Dan A. Blake.

# SAINTS: PLASTIC,
## ERRONEOUS,
### AND OTHERWISE

*J. D. Grey is pure gold. He is not a hypocrite. A hypocrite is one who may be mean, but he pretends to be good. If anything, J. D. is good and would make people think he is not so good.*

James L. Sullivan

*The Saints are the sinners who keep on trying.*

Robert Louis Stevenson

*I cannot praise a fugitive and a cloistered virtue, unexercised and unbreathed, that never sallies out and sees her adversary, but slinks out of the race, when that immortal garland is to be run for, not without dust and heat.*

John Milton

*I have always said: Paducah, Kentucky, can boast of three patron saints, Irvin S. Cobb, Alben W. Barkley and J. D. Grey.*

Frank Norfleet

*Real saints are hardly aware of this quality in themselves.*

Penrose St. Amant

*A man is free to breathe or not to breathe, but he doesn't lock himself up in an airtight room and stop breathing. It is the same way with religion. Religion is life.*

J. D. Grey

# VIGNETTE 1

*If you can dream—and not make dreams your master;*
*If you can think—and not make thoughts your aim.*

## SHADES OF GREY

A stranger in New Orleans in search of a saint would dare not confine the quest to a phone booth, yellow pages, and walking fingers. Nor would the stranger in search of a saint follow the advice of an articulate cab driver and look for a saint in black and gold on a proper Sunday in the Sugar Bowl stadium. Disappointed would be the searcher if he found himself deposited before a block of marble at the corner of *Walk and Don't Walk*. Saint-watching in the city would bring the same disappointment that a visitor in the city of New York experienced when he asked a cab driver to take him to the Church of God. When delivered to the steps of St. Peter's Cathedral, the passenger asked in all sincerity, "Is this the Church of God?" to which the cab driver replied, "Buddy, if He's not here, He's not in town." Although many of the cab drivers in New Orleans know J. D., not one of them would refer to him as a saint in the Crescent City. It is unfortunate, indeed, that down through history the saint-image has been so disfigured and distorted from the New Testament description of a real live saint.

Most people today had much rather be called a secular saint than a Christian saint. There was a time when people sought to leave the impression that they were better than they really were. Today many people seek to leave the impression that they are worse than they really are, one reason

**17**

being that they do not want to be known as "holier than thou" persons. Even the most devout ministers and laymen would flee from that title faster than a gray ghost ten seconds before daylight. "Saint" is not even a part of their vocabulary. The word has a curious history of ecclesiastical limitation. As used in the New Testament, it is a most inclusive term. The saints in Philippi, Corinth, and Rome, to whom the apostle addressed his epistles, were for the most part humble people, without position or distinction. They were not stars in the sky, but rather flowers sown by the hand of God in the common field. They were sincere, if imperfect, disciples of Christ, and to them was given the name "saints."

Yet when one moves into the history of the church, he discovers that the name was limited to those who had attained a distinction beyond the rank and file, or to those who supposedly possessed miraculous powers. Somewhere the idea was introduced that saints were the spiritual aristocrats. One of St. J. D.'s favorite stories is descriptive of the distortion of a saint in church history as compared with the saint in the New Testament. St. J. D. tells of a young baseball player who was trying to play left field. In his first game, he missed every ball that came in his direction. Finally, in disgust, the manager went out and took the glove away from the young man. Ironically, the first ball hit into left field rolled between the manager's legs. He went back to the dugout and said to the kid, "You've got left field so messed up, no one can play it."

Through the years critics have made light of the false image of saints. To illustrate:

"A saint is a dead sinner, revised and edited." Ambrose Bierce.

"There are only two kinds of men, the saints who think

they are sinners and the sinners who think they are saints."

"Saints are intolerant of sinners, but no more so intolerant than sinners just turned saints."

"Hell can have no terror for the poor sinner who has just gotten himself married to a saint."

J. D. is not a miracle worker even though some of his church members may think he is. Howard Jacobs in his column "Remoulade" in the New Orleans *Times Picayune*, penned under the subject "Miracle Worker":

The reputation of J. D. Grey as a doer and dynamic figure among the city's clergymen gives point to this incident which occurred the other evening at the First Baptist Church, of which he is pastor.

A little old lady approached the soft drink machine in the lobby and inquired of a group of men standing nearby whether anyone had change for a quarter. Nobody had, but one bystander suggested she put her quarter into the machine, and it would return twenty cents change.

"You're not serious," she said incredulously.

"Oh, yes, ma'am," he replied. "Here I'll show you." He took the quarter from her hand, deposited it in the machine, got in return a soft drink and twenty cents change.

"Well, I'll be hornswoggled," she exclaimed in astonishment. "Leave it to J. D. Grey to think of something like this."

It is constantly necessary to remind ourselves what real sainthood is. The current estimate is either too high or too low. Sometimes it is too high. There are those who classify saints with a lofty kind of piety, a people who belong in a class by themselves. Or again, the estimate is too low. A saint, to some, is one who thinks he is holier than others, a strange way of saying he thinks that he is holier than he is. G. K. Chesterton explained the aerodynamics of heavenly bodies by observing, "Angels can fly because they take themselves so lightly."

Brooks Hays used the occasion of a civic dinner tendered Grey in honor of his twenty-five years in New Orleans to relate the following story:

"Halloween had arrived and a little girl, a pre-schooler, was asked by her mother what she wanted to be when she went out to do her trick or treating. The little girl replied, 'I want to go as an angel.' So the mother went to work making a very elaborate angel costume for the little girl.

"On Halloween when the little girl put on her angel costume, she was a walking, talking dream. She started out on her trek from house to house. She was being 'Oh'd' and 'Ah'd' by everybody. Down the line she came to a home and knocked. The man who came to the door looked down at her in all her beauty and exclaimed that she was the prettiest thing he had seen. He had been seeing nothing but goblins and ghouls. He said, 'Now, what are you?' The little girl answered, 'I am an angel.' Then he said, 'What kind of angel are you?' She responded, 'I'm a little Baptist angel.' He said, 'Well, you are the most beautiful thing I ever saw, little Baptist angel. You stay here. I want to get you something special instead of this little penny piece of candy.' So he went back into the house and soon returned with a big, beautiful, delicious apple. He polished it and said, 'Now hold your little sack up here. Her eyes followed the apple as he dropped it into the sack of goodies; then she looked up at him and said, 'Now look at that—you broke every damn one of my cookies!' "

Perhaps, on the other hand, a saint could be defined as a person who possesses the negative virtues of meekness, humility, and resignation, but is short of the positive virtues of courage and daring. Evidently the New Testament saints belong to neither extreme. They were not weak and nervous people; rather, they were brave and forceful followers of

Jesus. Neither were they finished products. The apostles kept busy pointing out to them their faults and their failings.

What, then, were they? They were men and women who felt that they had been bought with a price and called to live pure and holy lives, expressing in them the gospel which they possessed as a precious treasure in their hearts. The New Testament presents no more moving spectacle than that of this faithful company of the saintly as they went about spreading the fragrance of dedicated living in the midst of the corruption of their times. They offer comfort and inspiration for all of us through their evidence of the possibility of the existence of real sainthood in the average man.

Into such a classification would we have to place J. D., with certain modifications; indeed, if he were classified, he would prefer a small *s*. This spelling of the title would lift the man out of the study and the stained-glass sanctuary and locate him in the neon-lighted cement jungle where the human animals toil, laugh, cry, doubt, and wonder. In the spelling of the word he is not a displaced refugee from men, for his ministry has not characterized him to be above or beyond, but *with* them—in the freest sense, living out the only kind of sainthood that really matters. He would be in the company of Menen, who observed: "I admire the saints because they were such uncompromisingly difficult people to get on with. My brother always says that it's a happy bishop who hasn't got a saint in his diocese."

The New Orleans archdiocese was present in the person of Archbishop Rummel at a city-wide function hosted by Mayor Victor Schiro and his councilmen. Two thousand citizens were on hand, and the nervous administration had requested three prayers to safeguard the silver. The Rabbi would pray. The Archbishop would pray. And the Saint would pray.

J. D. remembers the occasion as following closely on the twenty-fifth anniversary of his tenure in the city. The church had remembered the years in a special way by casting a medallion honoring their minister. With one of these in his pocket, J. D. arrived at the room where the celebrities, who would sit at the head table, were doctoring themselves with flu shots. The flu serum was not of the variety which the A.M.A. prescribes. Nor was it in the category that can be deducted as a medical expense.

"I usually go a little late," recalled J. D., who somehow had escaped the epidemic, "knowing what the pre-meeting function involves. I walked up and greeted the Archbishop. He shook my hand and I thought then he was sick, for his hand felt cold and wet. Then I realized he had only switched his drink from one hand to the other—a scotch and soda, I guess. I said, 'Your Excellency, I am so glad to see you.' He replied, 'I am glad to see you, Dr. Grey. Congratulations on your twenty-fifth anniversary at First Baptist Church.' Some nice compliments were exchanged, and I added, 'Well, thank you, sir. I regret your recent illness. I was in Baton Rouge one day and went by the hospital to see you, but the nurse said that you were not able to see anybody, so I left word. By the way, we Baptists don't believe in religious medallions like you Catholic brethren do; but some members of my flock had a special medallion struck on the occasion of my twenty-fifth anniversary. We call it the St. J. D. Medal. I want to give you one that I personally have blessed." With this, J. D. hauled out the medal from his hip pocket and gave it to the churchman. Grey's tidal wave of humor capsized the Archbishop's funnybone that in turn tilted the glass he held. The waves washed down his arms to his hand, and in a flash the newly-honored Saint was literally christened with scotch and soda. He is still uncanonized by the Catholic Church; but in a brief moment he was simultaneously baptized and saved from the flu epidemic.

The sign *A Saint at Work* to him would reveal a man serving God in the only way possible—serving others, taking his cue from Jesus, who came not to be ministered to but to minister. This free-wheeling, exasperated, lower-case saint frustrates attempts at canonization.

The devil's advocate would find many reasons to deny J. D. initiation into that select fraternity of sainthood—the debonair candidate with his clay feet in full view and his cigar firmly clenched in his fist. His speech is devoid of the musty clichés of traditional Christendom. His saint's sackcloth is free of the odors of piety that offend the spiritual nostrils of the man on the street. How can he be admitted if he will not play the saints' game according to the rules?

St. J. D. Grey—yes, his zip code is New Orleans, but he is at home in the Universe.

# RIGHT ANSWERS

## TO

# WRONG QUESTIONS

*Woe to you, men learned in the scriptures and Pharisees, actors on the stage of life, playing the role of that which you are not, because you pay a tenth of sweet-smelling garden-mint and anise seed and caraway seed, and have omitted the weightier matters of the law, the equitable administration of justice, and the mercy, and the fidelity. And these things you were obligated as a necessity in the nature of the case to have done, and not to have omitted those others. Blind guides, who by a filtering process strain out the wine-gnat, yet gulp down the camel.[1]*

The Gospels: An Expanded Translation [1]
by Kenneth S. Wuest


*J. D. Grey refuses to be intimidated by the "in" crowd or the contemporary pious style. Long before the young people invented the phrase, J. D. Grey insisted on "telling it like it is." He refused to pronounce sibilance whether moral, doctrinal, or ecclesiological just so he could be "kosher." He communicates a level of dedication to God which no one ever doubts because it is clear that he believes as least as much as he says. Obviously this shakes the establishment and shocks the people who identify religious depth with prissy piosity. But the man caught in the rough and tumble of life, struggling to be in the world but not of the world, immediately understands that J. D. Grey is the kind of Christian he could be where stained-glass office windows would be out of place.*

Duke McCall

# VIGNETTE 2

*If you can trust yourself when all men doubt you,*
*But make allowances for their doubting too.*

## SHADES OF GREY

It has been the observation of J. D. (Jabbing Defying) that some church members have a religion as false as their dentures and live and act as if they have no religious cavities but have reached the crest of perfection. In turn they adopt the ancient Pharisees' superiority complex and thank God for it—the complex that places them in the category of being better than others.

Men, like our pepper-and-salt Grey man, have always said, "It was to this group and their counterparts that Jesus saved His hardest words of condemnation." Such thoughts J. D. voices clearly: Jesus had no use for the pious-talking sinner, whether he was a Pharisee or downright phony; He could see through their charades and He knew what was in their hearts; He decried play-acting; He decried wearing of masks. To Him, in short, it was an appalling thing to turn religion into an act, a show, an outward observance with no inner dedication. He tore away masks and exposed artificiality and superficiality—the posing, pretending, play-acting. The Saint has observed that strict moralists never seem to run out of ideas about what others should do but rather insist that everyone adhere to the moralists' standards. It has been this prevalence of self-righteousness that has bred a practical atheism. Grey notes that if men are perfect, obviously there is no need for grace. Consequently,

sensible Grey matter would demand that the honest and
humble should attempt, as suggested by G. K. Chesterton,
"to squeeze out of its soul the last drop of the oil of the
Pharisees."

Jabbing Grey has contended vociferously that some folks
act more as if they are the disciples of the Scribes and the
Pharisees than disciples of Jesus Christ. These people are
legalists to the core, very much like the Scotchman playing
golf with an Englishman. When the Englishman suffered
a massive stroke on the course, the Scotchman made him
count it. If to puritanical minds all things are impure, then
says our crystal-gazing Grey, are they not following in the
footsteps of the Pharisee with the same foggy spiritual
nearsightedness—the Pharisee who thought the keeping of
the minutiae of religious ritual and ceremony more important than inner motives. Perhaps H. L. Mencken was
right when he said that the puritanical group have the
haunting fear that someone somewhere may be happy. Grey
maintains that many have either forgotten or have never
known how apparently blind the Pharisees really were in
legalistic attitudes even to the point of having the audacity
to complain about and condemn Jesus and His disciples
because they did not fulfill the ritualistic requirement of
handwashing before eating. Would they have dared suggest
that the disciples were unsanitary? Yet they contended
that they were unspiritual because they did not adhere to
the letter of ceremonial law. For the Pharisee, manners
came before motives, as our crystal-gazer stated, and there
was a reverence for negation which stymied spiritual development. Truly then, did not the Pharisees neglect the
inner motives of religion which give true Christianity its
meaning and significance? Does it follow then, our Saint

asks further, that the religion of the Pharisees was based
on what man can do, not on what God helps man to do?

Christianity is not that kind of religion, J. D. says emphatically. It has a different purpose, namely, to make men
to feel their need of God, their dependence upon Him. Men
cannot be Christians just by will power and determination,
by rolling up their sleeves and blowing on their hands.
Christianity then to this Grey man of God is a positive
persuasion rather than a list of negations. Unfortunately,
the mere mention of the top ten can mean only the Ten
Commandments. An invitation to come to the table is always interpreted as a reference to the sacred tables of the
law. The legalists give every appearance of being unac-
quainted with the eleventh commandment: "Thou shalt love
the Lord thy God with all thy strength, with all thy heart and
thy neighbor as thyself." Instead they seem to find the "shalt
nots" easier to obey than one great "thou shalt." All would
concur that to live up to the Ten Commandments, though
no small endeavor, is easier than the radical application of
the Sermon on the Mount.

To illustrate, various writers of history have related how
Southern slave-owners and Yankee slave-ship captains who
read their Bibles daily would have felt it a dangerous compromise to their Christian principles to do business about
their slaves on Sunday or let alcohol touch their lips. Remember that in the 1930's church members of the more
pietistic groups within the state churches of Germany
praised Hitler because he did not drink or smoke.

Nobody wants a negative religion, contends J. D., for
even those who have it are unhappy with it. The rich young
ruler who had kept all of the Commandments from his youth
up realized something was missing. "Reading between the
lines one can discern the bewilderment of the young man.

For he was obviously self-assured and thought of himself as good, for had he not 'kept the law from his youth up?' Therefore, his head must have spun when he heard, in reply to his courteous address, Jesus' quick rejoinder, 'Why do you call me good?' Had he not realized that there were all kinds of goodness, that some kinds are not worth much, and indeed some kinds are simply good for nothing? There is a goodness which is only skin deep; a goodness displayed for the sake of reputation; a goodness that confuses respectability with righteousness; a goodness that keeps the law but breaks the spirit of the law; a goodness that grows vain and in its vanity becomes cruel and condescending; a goodness that plays it safe behind every moralism and avoids inconvenience as if it were the plague; a goodness that is good within the patterns of the past but has no eye for the present evil; a goodness that clings to distant benevolences but is blind to the shrieking injustice of the crucifixion near at hand. Goodness is as corruptible as anything else. Once it is corrupted it tends to appear in its most impeccable assumptions." [2]

The Defiant Saint has pointed up again and again throughout his ministry the salient fact that Jesus had little use or patience for those small people, the professional moral critics who walk with a legalistic goose step, always ready to deplore the faults and sins of those around them, but who are incredibly blind to their own resistance to the grace and mercy of God. J. D. might well employ the words of the caustic Dean William Inge, who, when speaking of the bitter and the mean look of self-righteous persons, concluded, "We who know them on earth can understand that their appearance in heaven will not be greeted with enthusiasm." A Grey diagnosis would conclude that such an arthritic religious gait gives evidence of a stiffening of the spiritual joints, and would confirm the reflection that "goodness is harder to live with than badness unless it is a sane and balanced brand of goodness."

Shortly after J. D. was elected president of the Southern Baptist Convention a fellow preacher in Mississippi wrote him: "I had always admired you. I have heard you on the radio. I have heard you at the Convention. I have read a lot of your stuff, but somebody the other day told me that you smoked. I want you to tell me that it is not true. I can't believe it."

J. D. wrote back and said: "Dear Brother, thank you for your letter. Yes, you have been correctly informed. Occasionally I do enjoy a good cigar. But I tell you, if you don't smoke, I don't blame you a bit and I wouldn't criticize you because that is your business, and I wouldn't try to force you to smoke against your will. And if anybody ever does try to force you to start smoking, you let me know and I'll come to your defense. Thank you for writing. Yours truly, J. D. Grey."

*Some Fatherly Advice:*

"Shortly after coming to New Orleans I was in and out of the drug store at the Medical Arts Building near the Touro Hospital. An employee, a fine Catholic, whose brother owned the store, said to me one day, 'Reverend Grey, I hear these doctors in here call you Doctor Grey. Now I thought you were a reverend. How can you be a doctor and a reverend?' 'Well, Lucy,' I answered, 'about as easily, I guess, as your pastor, an old bachelor, can be called Father.' 'You ought to be ashamed of yourself!' she exclaimed. 'Well,' I said, 'you brought the subject up. Doesn't it figure?' She durst not ask me any more questions!"

*A Question from the Comfortable Pew*

"Not long after that the church was gathered on a Wednesday evening at prayer meeting and the congregation was granting letters. I was reading off a list of names of people and letters being granted. I said, 'All in favor of granting the motion, say *Aye*. All opposed, say *No*.' A loud 'No' startled the crowd. I didn't know who it was. Then he staggered up. He was a drunk who had slipped in and he continued, 'I don't object, Reverend, but, read the list again.' About that time two of the men who were there grabbed him and ushered him out. It was so tense you could hear a pin drop so I added, 'Anybody else want to raise a question about what we do in this church?' "

St. J. D. is not interested in second-rate questions; he is impatient with a question from the beaten path on which the Pharisees continue to walk and stumble. Rather, he is profoundly interested in the questions which reveal dimensions of concern and depth of insight, questions which affect man in his journey and the size of his world. What are the right questions? The ultimate questions? The questions on the boundary? Even Voltaire judged a man by his questions rather than by his answers. A child does not learn by asking questions but by getting the right answers to his questions. Some men, unfortunately, have many of the little answers, but have never even heard of some of the big questions. "We are impatient with mystery, skeptical of anything we cannot measure or isolate, all of which means we do not like questions framed in such a way as to make it difficult for us to find answers; we turn the questions around to fit the kind of answers we can find." [3]

Judicial Grey does not mean to imply that questions are unimportant. To him, it is essential that a man have a question. The question mark in our language may be the most authentic sign of our humanity. A man without a question is a contradiction of creation. It has been said by the late P. H. Anderson, "Any time you can lose your illusions and keep your faith, you are on the way." It is little wonder that our sage believes that any breakthrough to the light begins with a question asked in the darkness. Science has knocked down the walls of the laboratory; it has rent in twain the veils that hang in our universe. By their questions you shall know them. Further, is it not imperative that a man ask the right questions? Dead-end streets do indeed await those who fail to ask the right ones.

Evidently J. D. Grey believed, as has been said, that there are not fifty-two lessons; there are only five—God, man, sin, grace, eternity. The same holds true with our questions. There are only four major questions: "What am I (separated from creation)? Whose am I (separated from God)? Who am I (separated from self)? Why am I (separated from God)? In life, the Cross and the question mark are inextricably intertwined. These questions can be answered only in the light of biblical revelation, for man is the product, the problem, and the passion of God. J. D. Grey as a man knows through personal experience that human beings must learn to live with some unanswered questions. Who can hear Jesus cry in the darkness, "My Father, why?" and expect to bear His name with pat answers? J. D. (Job Dauntless) appearing before a Southern Baptist Pastors' Conference on crutches and admonishing the ministers not to become discouraged and give up said, "I'm not limping because I've been working out with the New Orleans Saints, though someone needs to work out with them; and it isn't Jim Garrison who made me this way. I'm not worried about Jim. I've lived through six district attorneys, three mayors, and three archbishops in New Orleans, and I'm still going. I have pastorized one church for better than thirty years. You ought to see how some of the members look. I've buried some of them."

In recent years Grey has felt like changing his name from J. D. Grey to Job D. Grey. "While recuperating from gastrectomy in the fall of 1967, I thought of this statement by Job's wife when she said, 'Curse God and die,' and I, Job, said back to her: 'No, no, I've got a few more benefits under my Blue Cross Plan, and I don't want to miss them.' "

Paul, who enjoyed using the term *saint* to describe a follower of Christ, lived with unanswered questions, one being the "thorn in the flesh" which was his constantly nagging companion. He wrote, "We are handicapped on all sides, but we are never frustrated; we are puzzled, but never in despair. We are persecuted, but we never have to stand it alone; we may be knocked down, but we are never knocked out."

One of J. D.'s fellow pastors, G. Avery Lee, after seeing him in a wheel chair at Moisant Airport, where they were both jetting out to the Southern Baptist Convention, penned this note to his own congregation: "In the past four years one of our Baptist preachers, Dr. J. D. Grey, has had much pain. He has had spinal surgery and other surgery, two cataracts removed, and is now afflicted with arthritis and often hospitalized for treatment. During all three ordeals, he has shown the good grace of an indomitable will. Some shields of gold have been removed, but it hurts me to see this robust man in a wheel chair at the airport enroute to Miami. Yet the brightness was there, and no man had any greater earlier chances than he. He has used his opportunities well. Now this one chance to show the radiance and the meaning of his faith is being used."

Like all great men in a world of questions, J. D. acts upon what answers he has. The Saint has manifested the faith of the poet who said, "Who draws one step through doubting dim, God will advance a mile through blazing light to him." The faith life always demands that the faithful act on piecemeal information. Man walks not by answers but by faith. On the walls of a cellar in Cologne, Germany, after World War II were found these words: "I believe in the sun even when it is not shining. I believe in love even when I feel it not. I believe in God even when He is silent."

A saint will face a thousand questions in a lifetime, most of them unimportant, beside the point, irrelevant. Yet saints have to answer—that's the name of the game. The question-raiser is forever in search of an answer man. If the saints can't tell us, who can?

# HOW TO
# BREAK UP A MEETING
# WITHOUT A RAID

*The man who sees the consistency in things is a wit . . .*
*The man who sees the inconsistency in things is a humorist.*

G. K. Chesterton

*J. D. Grey is a man with integrity of expression. He has*
*his convictions and will express them without hesitation. Yet,*
*he differs without letting differences destroy a friendship.*
*I know of no other who has his gift for keeping friends de-*
*spite disagreements.*

John J. Hurt, Jr.

*The Chinese have a story based on three or four thousand*
*years of civilization. Two Chinese coolies were arguing heat-*
*edly in the midst of a crowd. A stranger expressed surprise*
*that no blows were being struck. His Chinese friend replied,*
*"The man who strikes first admits that his ideas have given*
*out."*

Franklin Delano Roosevelt

# VIGNETTE 3

*If you can bear to hear the truth you've spoken*
*Twisted by knaves to make a trap for fools.*

## SHADES OF GREY

An occupational hazard for men in the public eye is the
ever-present nuisance of those who use meetings as opportunities to erect their own towers of Babble. J. D. (Jovial
Debater) is a one-man demolition team whose expertise is
well known. He can slip the cornerstone out of the storm-
cloud castles of such men, have those castles tumbling about
their ears, and make them like it.

Unfortunately for the uninitiated, there are no courses offered in institutions of higher learning, secular or theological,
which might be labeled "Philosophy for a Tense Moment"
or "Instant Upstaging." Those who have observed J. D.
through the years (some can show their scars) know that
he is a past master at waving the wand of humor. To him,
discord in a Baptist meeting house is noise out of place. He
believes Christians should learn to use the keyboard of life to
avoid the discords, but, more than that, they should go after
the harmonies. Gandhi said it for him, "God turns his back
on those who quarrel among themselves."

Disagreements are bound to come; they cannot be avoided
when one believes in putting into practice the priesthood of
every believer. "God save us," Grey says, "from the infalli-
bility of a private opinion." J. D.'s patience is stretched thin
when some people engage in debate to avoid thinking, especially when they enjoy the cathedral roll of their ministerial

**39**

accents—or when they enjoy the comfort of opinion without the discomfort of thought. Emerson sagely observed in his day: "A man in the wrong may more easily be convinced than one half right." Such men, according to Grey, insist on expressing their opinion as if it were the thought for the month or the ages. They are diehards who worship the ground their heads are in. All some men want to do is to give the bias of their opinions. With some it is easier to part with a friend than opinion. Their favorite calisthenic, jumping to conclusions, is not nearly so healthy as digging for the facts. George W. Truett sensed their presence in his own day as he said, "The great danger of the hour is feisty dogs and little men."

Jeremy Taylor observed in the 17th century: "Some people collect a bunch of thorns and sit down upon them." There are some computer-age thorn collectors who select the disagreeable things about any situation and dwell upon them to the exclusion of anything pleasant or hopeful. How does one effectively administer the rabies treatment to these perennial pests? There must be a pervading sense of fair play, even for those who ask for it. J. D.'s philosophy is: "Whenever you back a man into a corner, always leave him room enough to get out, and he will be eternally grateful to you for it." Spurgeon warned Mr. Tat-Tat, "You must not pat your arguments flat on to the crown of another man's hat." An arbitrator cannot adopt the stance of the mother-in-law who always favored one side in any dispute. It was the mother-in-law who sang

> In matters controversial
> My perception's rather fine;
> I always see both points of view—
> The one that's wrong, and mine.[1]

Another face which can be recognized through the prison windows of the tower of Babble is that of Cry-Now Pessimist. His contribution to the wail parade goes: "Last night I saw upon my stair a little man who wasn't there. He wasn't there again today. My God, I wish he'd go away." Through those same prison windows one catches a glimpse of Felton Fanatic. He has as much use in Baptist circles as a flabberstat on the ratastushus of the shishipah. As one sage wrote, "A fanatic is a lunatic with a hobby"; or as another said, "A fanatic is a man who would do everything God would do if God had all the facts." His solution, when he has forgotten his aim, is to redouble his efforts. In brief, there is often only a short step from the hypercritical to the hypocritical.

The Saint is vociferous in demanding that every man should be dedicated to being a part of the solution and not part of the problem. He has never led a protest or carried a placard, but he might if his placard read "BOYCOTT ALL PIMPLE PICKERS."

Is it not understandable that various Baptist leaders (the authors included) have confessed that whenever they find themselves in a skirmish they want J. D. (Jamming Demolishing) in their corner. G. Earl Guinn, president of Louisiana College, expressed it admirably at the celebration of Grey's thirtieth anniversary in New Orleans: "I feel toward J. D. Grey about like Winston Churchill felt toward his friend, the first Earl of Birkinghead. He said of him, 'If he was with you on Monday, he would be the same on Tuesday. And on Thursday when things looked blue, he would still be marching forward with strong re-enforcements.' I would rather have J. D. Grey at my side, cataracts, arthritis, and all, than 99 percent of the people in all this world."

*In Interview*

"J. D., how do you feel about Baptists washing their linen in public?"

"Well, I feel that all problems should be dealt with by proper agencies and in a proper manner without public display. I think of the experience of the Southern Seminary when they had their problems in the late fifties. At the time, I served with the committee of former presidents in working behind the scenes and in executive sessions with the brethren of divergent opinions. The committee poured oil on the troubled waters, worked the thing out, and thus resolved many of the problems. Of course, I would never be in favor of covering wrongdoing, violation of laws, and immoral acts, and I think little of the brethren who use the convention floor as a pillory upon which the people are criticized or suspended for public execution."

"Can you recall any situations which deteriorated into a brawl because you were unable to speak? Times when the barn door was left open?"

"Did I stay quiet on certain issues that were up? I don't think I have ever stayed quiet on anything that I really believed in. I have always had two principles I've tried to follow—one of them, if somebody else makes the point, let it be made. I sometimes have waited to see if somebody else is going to bring out a fact that I know and that others know. If they do not, then I will bring it out. The second thing is that I always want to be sure that I have my facts. I don't want to take off without getting my mule hitched up, as goes the expression."

"How far would you let a man go who keeps asking for it? What method would you employ before lowering the boom on him?"

"Well, I've never thought of that; I never thought of that.

I just sort of fly by the seat of my pants or wait for impressions to come up naturally. At times I know I've been criticized for maybe hitting too hard and sometimes dealing in personalities, though I didn't mean to be vicious about it or belittle a brother. But there are times you hear a man get up and debate on a thing that you know he doesn't believe down in his heart. He's told you in private the very opposite of what he is arguing for, but it looks as if he's been converted for some reason or other. Yet I have the feeling that he hasn't changed. I have said, 'Well, now, that is strange, Brother So and So. When we talked this matter over a couple of weeks ago, you didn't have this point of view. What's happened to make you change your mind?' And then and there I put him on the spot. In one or two cases, I've seen fellows back down from a position which I knew was not what they really believed.''

"Do most obnoxious people, from your observation, fit into a certain pattern? Do they exhibit certain traits? Are they seeking the limelight? Are they seeking attention?"

"Well, dealing with humanity in all relationships in every arena, not just in Baptist meetings, many times persons who ride a hobby-horse to death are frustrated individuals. When you really check into it, you find that they can't get along with anybody. Now a few times we have had people who cause trouble by criticizing established policies in the church. I find they have belonged to four or five or six other Baptist churches in the same city and that they have been troublemakers everywhere they have gone. I illustrate with this simple example. When I talk with a woman who is planning to divorce her husband, I become upset by the stories she tells me until I find she's been married three or four or five times already. Then I conclude that particular woman couldn't get along with any man. And I feel the same way about deacons

ess people or those in any other arena of activity.
llow a pattern of being incompatible and incongruous
and disagreeable—generally just a dern nuisance."

"Is there anything else you would like to add at this point
about how to break up a meeting without a raid? What are
some of the basic things you fall back on when a situation
is tense or you see that possibly it is going to get out of control?"

"Well, I think of course, anyone must have a sense of
humor. I've always felt when people are getting into debates
with stuff flying all over the room, and everybody is shouting
to be heard, that it's good when a soothing voice can be
heard or a change of pace given. Then people see how ridicu-
lous the thing is they are debating or arguing about and
realize it is not an important enough issue to break up fel-
lowships and disrupt the whole program.

"I remember in a deacons' meeting here a couple of years
ago, we had a fairly controversial issue up for debate, and
I thought I knew what the feelings of the majority of the
brethren were. Yet the minority was determined to be heard,
and rightly so. That was all right, and when they had their
say, there was a little lull. I smiled as broadly as I could and
said, 'Brother Chairman, I've been thinking in all of this discussion—and you could have heard a pin drop—I've been
thinking of a beautiful philosophy that I heard not long ago
that I think will give up guidance: Wet birds never fly at
night.' I paused for a moment, and again you could have
heard a pin drop. I repeated, 'Yes, wet birds never fly at
night.' Then I sat down leaving them completely bewildered
and befuddled. Well, I had heard this crazy Jackie Vernon on
television a few nights before use that expression with a
straight face, and he went on to say that 'my old grand-
father used to say it and I never knew what he meant, but

it impressed me.' As the meeting broke up, the deacons left in an amicable spirit. Later several men came to Jinks Mahnker, my secretary, and said, 'What did the pastor mean by that—wet birds never fly at night?' Some of the men thought that I was criticizing them, and that I was using something that had a hidden meaning to it. She laughed and said that they'd just have to ask the pastor what he meant. I never did explain it, and I never will.

"It's like the young fellow who when preaching on election got so involved that he said, 'You think I'm in water over my head, and I can't get out of this. I will show you I can. Let's stand and have the benediction!'

"Just walk off and leave it! That's just as good a way as any. Personally, I don't like to go down the hall debating with people when something has been settled in a meeting. Now when I was president of the Convention, I never let a man, I don't care how big he was, grab me outside in the hall or down at the hotel lobby to try to argue with me about decisions that were made or something I had done. I always said, 'Brother, that meeting is adjourned. If you want to bring it up tomorrow, bring it up. But I am not going to try to debate it right now or try to justify the rulings I made. As far as I am concerned, it's been said and that's it.' "

"Do you feel sometimes that a festered wound should be lanced on the spot, or do you administer healing oil?"

"Time gives the answer just as it did when my twins were growing up. They would get all excited about things, and I would say, 'Well, we'll see about it, we'll see . . .' Time is a great healer. You take a stream that is stirred up after a rain or shower—there's no way to settle it. There's no use bailing that water out. Just give it time and it will settle itself."

## Upstage

"Repartee has been defined as saying what you think after becoming a departee; saying as quick as a flash what you didn't say until the next morning. Everyone, at one time or another, has had occasion to echo the familiar lamentation:

> Backward, turn backward, O Time, in your flight,
> I've just thought of a wisecrack I needed last night!

"How often have you felt the need at a given moment for a whimsical wisecrack or a waggish quip to put a spark in your conversation? Why be caught with your gags down? You can't win in a battle of wits unless you are properly armed with a repertoire of rapid-fire repartee, a capsule caricature, a salty sally, or a snappy comeback." [2]

## Up-Stage

J. D. is at his best upstage, but experience has been his best teacher, for even the master quipper has been upstaged. During his days as a seminary student, the famed wit and humorist I. E. Gates came as guest chapel speaker. Following the service Cadet Grey presented his colors and challenged, "Dr. Gates, I know the book from which you got every word of that sermon." Calmly, Dr. Gates withered him with, "Young man, if I were as stupid as you, I would study the dictionary every day." J. D.'s Grey-matter has expanded awesomely since then, and from that day until this, strong men have cringed at the way in which the naive have challenged the Colonel. So many have been caught with their plans down.

St. J. D. has a special penchant for and also a delight in responding to introductions that have been a bit rough on him, especially in cases of a toastmaster who is a smart aleck. For instance, "Thank you, Mr. Task Master! Your introduction reminds me of the time a hungry lion caught an old donkey and announced he was going to eat him. The donkey said, 'Now, Mr. Lion, I am old and tough and you wouldn't enjoy eating me. Let me make a deal. I will go out into the valley and begin braying. That will frighten the rabbits, squirrels, foxes, and other small animals. Then you will have a juicy meal that you will enjoy.' The lion took up the proposition and said, 'Now don't fool me. I'll still get you if you don't do it.' Whereupon the donkey went down into the valley and began braying. Sure enough, here came all the little animals and the lion got his fill. Then he met the donkey and said, 'It really worked. You certainly frightened them. In fact, you would even have scared me if I hadn't known it was a jackass.' "

*Downstage*

When Grey is on the line, he is definitely downstage and plays his role as only a real trouper can. Through many years it has been J. D.'s policy to be in his study before the phone rings. Occasionally, he makes calls to church members before the working day begins. Early one winter morning he dialed a number he thought to be that of one of the men of the church. An unfamiliar sleepy voice answered. J. D. (Jovial Discerning) inquired, "Is this 921-8849?" The strange voice coldly retorted, "No! This is 921-8840." Quick as a dial tone, Grey said, "Friend, you have just picked up the wrong telephone!"

*On Stage*

Every man spends lost hours delivering brilliant rejoinders to yesterday's jabs. But J. D. is at his best on stage, even if the script is misplaced and the performance must be impromptu.

Scene: A Southern Baptist Convention Executive Committee meeting. The curtain opened on an emotionally charged group of ministers. The only things left to exchange were punches. Harsh words flew back and forth, elevating the temperature and accelerating cardiac conditions. J. D. took it all as long as he needed; then he broke up the meeting with, "Now that the brethren have given their devotionals, here are the real issues."

Scene: The Southern Baptist Convention meeting in Houston in 1953. The Booz, Allen and Hamilton report was under discussion, and the section covering the future of the Home Mission Board was up for debate. Things looked grim before J. D. (Joe DiMaggio) Grey, came to the plate and cleaned the bases. "Brethren, it looks to me like we are trying to kill the Home Mission Board, which has been the mother of most of us; and if this is going to be Mother's funeral, I want more than a shirt-tail full of people here this afternoon to debate this Booz, Allen and Budweiser report." This remark convulsed the assembly. A brother from Texas rose and spoke at length about the report coming from Booz, Allen and Hamilton. The raging waves subsided—the hawks folded their wings and bowed out.

Scene: The Southern Baptist Convention meeting in San Francisco in 1962. Professor Ralph Elliott had written a book, *The Message of Genesis*, which had become the center of a hurricane of emotion. Grey employed a backstage approach, though not by design. Standing at the back of the platform, watching the upheaval and listening to the verbal fireworks, he was approached by a half-dozen messengers in near panic who urged, "Go up there, Dr. Grey, and get us out of this mess—straighten it out." Grey turned and said, "Brethren, we've got so many saviors of this convention we're going to hurt somebody in trying to save it."

Perhaps he was recalling the words of one who said: "Burning stakes do not lighten the darkness."

Scene: Southern Seminary during an institutional crisis over an ultimatum issued by the faculty "committee of thirteen." George Ritchey relates that he was on the Board of Trustees at the time. "We had one meeting of trustees, some faculty members, and administration. Late in the night J.D., who was serving on the advisory committee of former SBC presidents, stood up and said: 'I did not attend this seminary, but it belongs to Southern Baptists, and I support it. I believe this is the time to practice our theology of reconciliation. Everybody involved in this situation is Christian, and it seems to me that Christians should resolve their differences.' He made a strong appeal for Christian attitudes and determination to settle difficulties as Christian men." So you have Grey the dove.

Scene: The Southern Baptist Convention meeting in Houston in 1953. The out-of-town reviews prepared the messengers for a stormy session. The focal point of the impending controversy was a report submitted by the Committee on Relations with Other Religious Bodies. J. D recalls: "In prior years this committee had presented its report to a strong chorus of discussion. There were some good recommendations in the report, which were acceptable to the vast majority present. But there were many among these who objected that the committee was too authoritarian in demanding that the Southern Baptist Convention be a body to exact doctrinal positions and enunciate them. We were not a body that would issue edicts and encyclicals because of the democratic structure of the convention."

The official minutes of the convention with President Grey presiding reveal the progress of the play:

145. T. C. Gardner, Texas, presented the report of the Committee on Relations with Other Religious Bodies and moved the adoption of Recommendations 1 and 2 as follows:

Recommendation No. 1

That the teaching agencies of the Convention continue their effort with renewed vigor to strengthen Baptist conviction with reference to the dangers of interdenominationalism and non-denominationalism.

Recommendation No. 2

That the Southern Baptist Convention through its teaching agencies continue to cooperate with the churches affiliated with our Convention in magnifying the scriptural, authoritative position of local, sovereign New Testament churches, defined in the constitution of the Southern Baptist Convention as 'Regular Baptist churches' in administering the church ordinances.

E. D. Solomon, Florida moved as amendment that the committee be continued for another year.

146. Walter Pope Binns, Missouri, moved, and it was carried that the time be extended fifteen minutes to allow for discussion.

147. The motion to continue the committee was discussed by Judson G. Jackson, Georgia, and Walter Pope Binns.

148. Chairman Van Arsdale called for the order of the day. Motion carried.

149. T. Rupert Coleman, Virginia, moved the Convention reconvene at 2:30 today to continue the discussion. Motion was lost.

150. Chairman Van Arsdale called for a special order of business at 9:30 tonight to continue the discussion. Motion carried.

J. D. picks up the threads of the story once again: "Then the discussion started, and finally it was agreed to set a special order to discuss the motion that night at 9:30. Well, when the afternoon papers came out, they were all predicting that Southern Baptists faced their first split, indicating that we were going to be split wide open and our fellowship torn up. I had a conference with Brother E. D. Solomon, and he was very disturbed about the matter. He said, 'You know, beloved (and I had known Brother Solomon, incidentally, since I was just a young fellow. I was his mother's pastor in Texas, and pastored two of his brothers and one of his sisters). I wouldn't want to cause any trouble at this convention. Do you feel that maybe it would be best for us not to continue the committee? If you think so, I will go in and ask that my motion to continue the committee be withdrawn.' I said, 'Brother Solomon, I believe it would be a great service to the Convention.' "

House lights dimmed. The curtain rose once more in convention hall.

175. The time for the special order of business having arrived, the Chair recognized E. D. Solomon, Florida, who asked for the privilege of withdrawing his motion made earlier in the day (See Item No. 145). The motion was withdrawn by unanimous consent.

176. T. C. Gardner and R. E. Milam, Oregon, spoke concerning the two recommendations embodied in the Report of the Committee on Relations with Other Baptist Bodies. Three recommendations were adopted. (See Item No. 145).

177. On motion of Perry Webb, the Convention gave a vote of thanks to the Committee on Relations with Other Baptist Bodies, which concluded its work with the adoption of the above report.

Following the vote of 177 the house fell silent again. What then followed was one of the most extraordinary moments in the official life of the Southern Baptist Convention, over a century old, as the president, our man from New Orleans, addressed the messengers in a brilliant display of spontaneous and extemporaneous common sense. President Grey's speech, from a tape recording of that session, follows, along with the concluding moments of the convention.

"May the Chair be indulged this: I am so sorry to disappoint you good people of the press over here. [Prolonged applause] But I will give you a story.

"Let it be said that Southern Baptists are an example of one of the finest of a pure democracy on the face of God's green earth. [Prolonged applause]

"Let it be said that the six divisive issues predicted would split this Convention; we have, after fraternal, brotherly, discussion, talking ourselves out, gone through them without any splits whatsoever. [Prolonged applause]

"Let it be said that Southern Baptists in their Convention and through their churches still follow what the First Baptist Church of Jerusalem followed when they said 'We will select a successor to take Judas' place,' and no ecclesiastical hierarchy said, 'I appoint you,' but they voted on the man they wanted. [Applause]

"Gentlemen, gentlemen of the *Washington Star*, the *Dallas News*, the *Atlanta Constitution* and *Journal*, the *Fort Worth Star Telegram*, and all the rest; say to the world that Southern Baptists still believe in doing what the First Baptist Church of Jerusalem did when they selected six deacons not by an ecclesiastical hierarchy picking out the men, but they voted on it among themselves and they were selected. [Prolonged applause]

"Let it further be said in the columns of the papers tomorrow, if they raise questions about Southern Baptists scrapping, that a Baptist Church in Old Virginia pastored by Dr. Tribble gave to Thomas Jefferson an example of what he thought to be the best form of government for these United States, a pure democracy. [Applause]

"Let it be said that if our forefathers left the shores of Europe with its political dictatorship and ecclesiastical imperialism to establish a democracy in this land, we have it in our life today in America. [Prolonged applause]

"And if it took the Congress of the United States three weeks to debate the question of the tidelands issue, when they finally came to vote to give the right to the tidelands oil to the states—as, bless the Lord, it ought to be all along—if it took them three weeks to debate and get there, wouldn't you let us Southern Baptists debate about 30 minutes on a thing as important as this? [Prolonged applause]

"And any other religious press, any yellow sheet or rag anywhere, that has been hoping that this Convention would be split from Dan to Beersheba, from Timbuktu to Kalamazoo; go back and tell them we know more about how our business is run than they know. [Amens—Prolonged applause]

"And every would-be prophet that talks much but knows little about what Southern Baptists are going to do on this and on that and on the other is just talking through his hat, and it's wishful thinking. And then go back to those who call Southern Baptists the problem child of Protestantism, and say to them that this is a democracy. [Amens—Prolonged applause]

"And anyone who would presume to dress down this Convention on its stand on various issues, say to that beloved brother, in all deference and respectability, that Southern Baptists know what they want to do and we are not mad at others in this world. We just don't want to put on the uniform and play on the team always exactly according to their terms, but we'll be pitching just the same. [Amens—Prolonged applause]

"When Tom Holloway presented the report the other night of the American Bible Society, my heart swelled within me when I had the record from the headquarters that Southern Baptists last year gave the second largest amount of money to the American Bible Society. [Applause]

"And when the President of the National Temperance League is a Southern Baptist—Dr. Duke McCall—I say to you that Southern Baptists take second place to no group of Christians today in the world for standing up and facing up and bearing their responsibility for carrying on our way of life in America under our democracy. [Applause]

"When Dr. Joe Dawson gave his report tonight, I wanted to say of him that he and Southern Baptists, along with others to be sure, stopped in its tracks the abortive attempt of the late but not always lamented President Truman to nominate an ambassador to the Vatican. [Prolonged applause]

"And say to your readers tomorrow, ladies and gentlemen, that Southern Baptists know what they want to do under God, and we are going to stay together and we are going forward to His glory. [Amens—Prolonged applause]

"And to any little, sweet, pietistic person who feels this Convention should be conducted like a prayer meeting and nobody raise his voice, let us say to him that we must discuss these issues. This is not a Wednesday night prayer meeting, nor an eleven o'clock service on Sunday morning. To some who have said we have made them nervous by a little bit of moving around, let us say, brethren, we will discuss these issues! We have to discuss them, and when we have our say out, we have our own scraps and then go our way; but we don't want anybody else jumping on us—we'll do our own jumping on one another. [Prolonged applause]

"If anything needs to be said further, though I doubt it [prolonged laughter] we will."

"Brethren," said Dr. E. H. Westmoreland: "I would like to make a motion and that is that this second edition of the President's address be printed also along with the first one." [Laughter —Prolonged applause]

Dr. Grey: "The motion is out of order because the constitution says they have to be printed before they are presented to the Convention, and this hasn't been printed. I doubt it could be printed." [Laughter—Prolonged applause] "But I dare say parts of it will be." [Laughter]

Westmoreland: "It's on tape recorders back behind here; we can get every word of it." [Laughter, prolonged laughter, and applause]

"We will be back in the morning at 9:30. You reporters come back now; we might have something for you in the morning. [Laughter—Prolonged applause] We are going to have a film tonight on temperance. What's the subject, Dr. Pollard?"

Dr. Pollard: "There is to be a very very remarkable show here at the conclusion of this service. All of you are invited to stay." [Dr. Grey—hammering gavel]

Dr. Grey: "Just a moment now! Just a moment now! The critics who want this to be an eleven o'clock church service or a funeral will say, 'They had disorder more like a political convention than anything else.' We still know what we are doing."

"We are going to pray as we go. Brother, what's your name?"

"Alvin M. Douglas."

"Will you come and lead us in the closing prayer?"

178. Alvin M. Douglas, Texas, led the closing prayer.

It was generally agreed by close friends and observers that J. D. had detoured around a possible Baptist brawl to the safe up-country level of a laugh-in.

Remembering the event from the relative objectivity of the turning years, J. D. states, "I feel, that I am not egotistical in saying this, that I was in a peculiar position to say these things and to get this committee discharged, because I was known as a rock-ribbed Southern Baptist, fundamentalist, a J. R. Graves—I. N. Pennick—J. N. Hall-type Baptist on doctrine, and I had the friendship of the conservative element. Yet if we have any liberal brethren they knew I was fair. I had enunciated in my presidential address at Miami the year before that the Southern Baptist Convention is not about the business of issuing edicts and encyclicals and demanding that the obedience of the churches be given in order to stay in the Convention. I aborted an attempt by a messenger from Texas to amend the constitution at the Miami convention when he came, about the next to the last day, and said he was proposing a constitutional amendment that membership be only for those churches which did not accept alien immersion and which practiced closed communion. I ruled this out of order because I said the constitution requires that these amendments shall be presented not later than the second day of the Convention. When he questioned my ruling I said, 'Would you appeal your ruling then to the Convention?' and he said, 'Yes, I appeal the ruling.' So I put it to the Convention. 'Would you sustain the president in ruling his notice of intention to amend the constitution out of order, or would you not?' They sustained it by an overwhelming voice. Very few voted against it, so it was in that frame of reference that I came into the Houston convention feeling that it would help our fellowship and not do any violence to the truth and our position as

Baptists if the Gardner Committee could be thanked and discharged."

The strong wording in the "Second Presidential Address" concerning irresponsibility among the press raised a few eyebrows, especially among the fourth estate. Grey smoothed some nervous newsmen later with "I did have in mind the editors of some of these yellow sheets of the Frank Norris variety that had always been criticizing Southern Baptists. I honestly did not have our own Southern Baptist press in mind or the reputable established secular press, the daily newspapers; but I was going so fast speaking without a manuscript that I didn't make my breaks in sentences and paragraphs clear. Some of the newsmen concluded I was pummeling everybody in general. Well, a few of my close friends said I was a little bit hard on the press, and some of my friends said I gave the press just what they were asking for. I still don't regret that the Second Presidential Address was given."

# NOW, BRETHREN!

*Codgers to the right of them*
*Whippersnappers to the left of them.*
*Codgers and whippersnappers in front of them.*
    *Into the jaws of death,*
    *Into the mouth of Hell,*
    *Ride the clergy!*[1]

Robert A. Raines

*J. (Joyful) D. (Disturbing) Grey! Defying all analysis, he moves on across the decades, lifting the burdened, stabbing awake the complacent, inspiring the alert.*

*"How old is J. D.?" someone asked. I quickly answered: "As old as the Gibralter of Wisdom; as young as the Morning's Dawn."*

*He walks the dusty lanes with a brother's touch for every neighbor, and every step is ordered by a heart of love and understanding.*

*He opens God's Book with reverent hand, and reflects its radiant mood and message to every listening soul.*

*He is aware of two worlds at one and the same time, ministering to the present in terms of the eternal.*

*He has blessed my life—Joyful Disturbing Grey, and I give thanks unto God upon every remembrance of his friendship.*

Louie D. Newton

*I have been with J. D. Grey in the First Baptist Church, New Orleans, on three different occasions, including a revival. I found him to be a very warm-hearted, spiritually sensitive, and uncompromising defender of the Faith and preacher of the Gospel.*

Warren C. Hultgren

# VIGNETTE 4

*If you can force your heart and nerve and sinew*
*To serve your turn long after they are gone.*

The platform manner of the silver-toned Grey resembles the flamboyant Dewitt Talmadge by virtue of his impressive head and strong physique. His outspoken style is reminiscent of Henry Ward Beecher—sometimes thundering, sometimes pleading, with a strong personality that dominated any platform he ever mounted, and a magnetic appeal that focused all eyes on him when he spoke. Beecher had unusual platform presence and the ability to command the attention of any audience. His voice was forceful and strong but always tinged with a note of humor characteristic of his personality. He used many clever phrases, but he was not simply a phrase-maker nor a stylist. He understood that, in the words of the apostle Paul, "unless I bring you something from God's revelation, what good do I do you?" (I Cor. 14:12, John Knox translation)

Pulpiteer Grey as a man of mature logic has developed his sermons through the years from a soberly reasoned and carefully thought out position. He has known that preaching is in fearful jeopardy when the raison d'être of the preacher is inarticulate.

He has been careful to begin by getting the attention of his audience, sometimes with a clever story, sometimes by a humorous remark or forceful description, but always first bridging the gap between the secular mind and the biblical world. Although he has incorporated richly biblical mate-

59

rials within his sermons, he has not been one of those preachers "who believed that people really came to church to find out what happened to the Jebusites." Although Grey may tell his congregation what happened to the Jebusites, he always concludes with a "But now, Brethren." His content has been scripturally oriented with a point. Even though it is good to know theology, Grey does not rattle its bones.

Some preachers seem to hold an audience by the sheer force of their personality, even if they have nothing to say. "The trouble with many preachers," complains J. D., "is that they have only one style. They are as unvarying in their style as they are in their attire, blue serge. They should adopt a style that varies—one adaptable to the occasion." When one sees a man who combines personality, style, and content to interest the modern secular mind, one has found an unusual combination or a charismatic one—color him Grey.

The Grey Bishop of New Orleans learned much from M. E. Dodd, former president of the Southern Baptist Convention, first preacher on the Baptist Hour, and a Shreveport minister of the first church in America to own and operate its own radio station. Hearing him first as a teen-aged boy, Grey says warmly: "He impressed me tremendously. Dodd was the greatest man I had ever heard speak." Dodd believed in a solidly Biblical approach to preaching, but he also had a gift for oratory and direct appeal to his congregation. Like his early idol, so does "Timothy" Grey. If being Biblical means being doleful and dour, then J. D. G. does not qualify. If being Biblical means taking life seriously, at the same time understanding and appreciating the breadth of all its vigorous and humorous aspects, then J. D. G. definitely qualifies as truly Biblical.

George W. Truett also left his mark on J. D. Frequently,

Grey has recalled: "When I first saw him, heard his voice, his tone and method—I jokingly said to other ministers that I believed George W. Truett could stand up and recite 'Mary had a little lamb; its fleece was white as snow'; and ten people would walk down the aisle to join the church." Grey proudly states, "I got my heart emphasis and compassion—what little bit I have—surfaced by the influence of Truett and Dodd. Many have contributed to my life. From L. R. Scarborough I got my desire for evangelism and missions as well as denominational loyalty and cooperation. He impressed me most in these areas. When I first heard R. G. Lee, I wished then to be flowery, graphic, and dramatic, for I felt his power and influence deeply."

Some people regard prophetic preaching as foreseeing the future, that is, as looking into a ministerial crystal ball and predicting the outcome of things. In that sense, J. D. has been neither a prophet nor the son of a prophet. If, on the other hand, prophetic preaching means *forth*telling in the Biblical manner rather than *fore*telling, then he has been prophetic indeed. He has been fearless in his proclamation, never afraid to strike a blow whether at some cherished sacred cow or at some secular institution that needed challenging.

It can be said without reservation that few pulpits have been as involved in the life of the city as the pulpit of the First Baptist Church of New Orleans. Perhaps one of the most prophetic preachers of all times was Savonarola in the city of Florence, Italy. Deeply involved with the Word of God, he was also deeply involved with the life of the city, a city in many respects very similar to New Orleans, cultured and pampered. Like Florence, New Orleans required a pastor who could live in the midst of a fun-loving city and at the same time challenge it prophetically to its very core.

Preaching, to the Saint, should be more illuminating than the gray of dawn. He believes in the prophecy of the pulpit and the centrality of preaching as an act of worship. He concurs with the famed preacher from Scotland, James S. Stewart, who said, "Preaching exists not for the propagation of views, opinions and ideals, but for the proclamation of the mighty acts of God." [2] To the Saint, great preaching has always been like a sword with two edges. On the one hand, it has taken seriously the historical revelation of God in Christ; it has attempted, on the other hand, to translate the implications of that message into the vernacular of its time. His preaching has sought to interpret these historical implications of God's acts in the midst of his people or any assembly which he has addressed. It has sought to encourage those same acts on the part of his contemporary disciples. J. D. G. has taken seriously that historical revelation, and, equally seriously, the need to translate its implications into the contemporary idiom, unlike that young Oxford graduate who, having only recently assumed his first pastorate, startled his congregation of charwomen and chambermaids by the rhetorical question: "Some of you probably are saying by now, 'So much for Cyril of Jerusalem but what about Philip of Mobsuestia?' "

Such remote theological ramblings are foreign to the Grey approach. Instead he shares J. B. Phillips' thoughts: "For many years it has been my solid purpose to communicate the truth of the Christian Gospel. I am not concerned to distort or dilute the Christian faith so that modern undergraduates, for example, can accept it without a murmur. I am concerned with the truth revealed in and through Jesus Christ. Let the modern world conform to him, and never let us dare to try to make him fit into our clever-clever modern world.

I do not care a rap what the 'avant-garde' scholars say; I very much care what God said and does." [3]

To the silver Grey, the Bread of Life should never, never be served up as a stale loaf; rather, it should have the tantalizing appeal of a load of bread fresh from the oven with no traces of a synthetic yeast. In short, a minister's goal in preaching should be excellence. J. D.'s high school principal set the limits of his horizons broadly when he advised, "Do not be satisfied too early or with small accomplishments." To paraphrase Oscar Wilde, a minister should have simple tastes—it should take the best to satisfy him.

For any minister the pulpit should be a first love as it is for J. D. Grey; but like J. D., a minister should love the people more than he loves to preach, for it is their needs and the press of the Word upon their needs that drives him to the pulpit again and again. In his pursuit of excellence in the proclaiming of the gospel, a minister should barricade mediocrity and never give it a password (any form of rationalization) to invade the horizon of his mind. At no time, according to Grey, should a preacher allow himself to become an inhabitant of the wasteland of meaningless activity. Being obsessed with meaningless activity prevents the minister from performing his primary task as a pastor in equipping the saints for their pastoral ministry. There is enough irritating noise in the world without the sermon's being "full of sound and fury, signifying nothing." In preaching, the minister should put the message across with life, with sincerity, in a direct eyeball-to-eyeball fashion: so insists the grey man.

*How to Build Bridges Across Credibility Gap*

Crossing Spiritual Wilderness has been the despair of many preacher pioneers. They have encountered and suffered in Dismal Swamp and the Desert of Ignorance. Indeed, nothing has claimed as many victims as the task of constructing lasting bridges over Credibility Gap. The chasm abounds with unfinished or wrecked attempts, and the rocky floor of that treacherous gorge contains the sad evidence of men who believed they had built bridges, but once they tried to transport weighty ideas across, their flimsy attempts gave way.

The Kentucky frontiersman, Davy Crockett Grey, has earned his reputation for straight shooting, perseveracity,* and building strong and lasting bridges across fearsome Credibility Gap.

The Saint is a discerning and uncompromising contractor when it comes to gathering his materials for bridge building. His experienced eye sorts out the counterfeit from the effective. Artificial bait may be effective in fishing, but artificiality is unacceptable in preaching. In an age of unbelief the audience may react in the same manner as the mountaineer who, when hearing a radio announcer predict rain, objected: "You can't never trust a weather report that comes over one of these here cheap transistor radios."

No one is more aware than Articulate Grey that this is an age of unbelief and that the people in the age of unbelief have found a chasm, uncrossable, between themselves and the object of spiritual truth. What hidden streams have rutted out the Credibility Gap? A stream of manipulating words has washed down from the snow job of the Mount Olympus of the advertising world, Madison Avenue. Grey addresses himself to people who are well accustomed to being conned by the hour over the boob tube. No one really believes

---

* *Perseveracity* is a Grey word to describe the attitude of the old hunter B. B. Crimm tells about. He discovered a nesting spot in an ancient tree and shouted, "Boys, let's keep shooting in that hole and see if there's a squirrel in it."

that success and sexuality are just a sweet breath away! Advertising's easy panaceas have created a credibility gap for all the users of words—even the users of The Word. It is no longer enough for a man to let down the tailgate of his ministerial medicine wagon and offer up his patent-medicine prescriptions to the half-smart rubes: the rubes have gone to school, and they have heard all the words—over and over and over, ad nauseam. Where are the guarantees of the efficacy of the miracle cure for the ails of the soul the pitch man dispenses so glibly? Does his gospel carry the *Good Housekeeping* seal of approval? Some sermons are rather like commercials in which you cannot tell if God is the product or the sponsor. The phony word merchants have even sent the radio and television executives scurrying for religious programming of integrity. They know the pressure from paid religion—including the almost overwhelming flood of hate-spreading, money-seeking, health-selling programs that distort and disgrace the Christian faith. Someone has observed that the Sermon on the Mount has been reduced to several trivial words and has suffered in the reduction.

"The proclaimer of the Word must be relevant in his words," advises Grey. "He should know the language of his people and try to speak according to their understanding. He should be lofty and speak in the language of the Book, but he must be able to communicate with his people. He should be like a boy who writes his girl a letter and underscores every word of it. It is better to present your ideas, however few, in an appealing manner than to know a lot and tell it poorly." The translator, J. B. Phillips, has said it for the man of Grey words, "If words are to enter men's hearts and bear fruit, they must be the right words shaped cunningly to pass men's defenses and explode silently and effectively within their minds." [4]

On the opposite side of the street you are prone to hear a version other than that advocated by J. D. "I know you believe you understood what you think I said, but I am not sure you realize that what you heard is not what I meant." This sends you rushing over the bridge where Socrates, as a translator of life, said to a young man, "Speak that I may see thee." Nothing, according to Grey, so reveals the inner quality of man as the words he utters when he opens his mouth.

A single inscription, "Preacher of the Word of God, Lover of Mankind," on the base of the statue of Phillips Brooks in Boston, points to the missing page in the plans of too many architects of the faulty bridges across Credibility Gap. Christians, cautions Grey, must be faithful to the Word of God and fall in love with mankind and the breath-taking age in which we live. "In the work of bridge-building—in the work of reconciliation, we must never lose heart," he says.

*On the Podium and Behind the Lectern*

In a major address at Southern Baptists Pastors' Conference, the subject of J. D. (Joking Deriding) was "Epitaphs on Preachers' Tombstones." Operating on the principle that for men to laugh at themselves is to see themselves, he did not deliver a knockout blow, but numerous short jabs to the ribs—some tickled, some stung! It was salt-and-pepper Grey all the way.

Through his ministry he has flown storm-warning flags to preachers and offered sugar-coated prescriptions of advice, not as if he had apprehended but as a companion in the rowboats, with the attitude of the Old Kentuckian who was celebrated for his sagacity. One day a young man asked him, "Uncle Zeke, how does it come you're so wise?" "Because," replied the sage one, "I've got good judgment. Good judgment comes from experience, and experience—well, that comes from poor judgment."

Grey has paid off his I.O.U.'s to an earlier generation of men by his continuing encouragement to the young ministers of today. Billy Graham was a collector of this generational debt, for he said, "Through the years Dr. Grey has done more than any other man to help me get established with Southern Baptists."

The late Roland Q. Leavell, after his retirement as president of New Orleans Baptist Theological Seminary, said to one of the authors: "We have invited J. D. to the seminary campus every year, and he has always done a good job in speaking to students. He has always been timely and has said things young ministers ought to hear and know. He has been practical and skilled in sharing his experiences with fellow preachers."

## Your Halo Fits Too Tight

"I get tired of these brethren who feel they've got to have that pious, holy tone," Deriding Grey exclaims. "I agree with Spurgeon: 'The vice of the ministry is that ministers will parson-ificate. We must have humanity along with our divinity, if we would win the masses. Everybody can see through affectations, and people are not likely to be taken in by them. Fling away your stilts, brethren, and walk on your feet; doff your ecclesiasticism, and array yourselves in truth.' "

> The Devil did grin
> For his darling sin
> Is Pride that apes humility.
> Coleridge

A minister tells how he met a friend in the terminal airport, and he noticed a new spring in his step. The friend said, "I have just resigned as general manager of the universe. It is amazing how swiftly the resignation was accepted." A companion temptation to playing God is the danger of losing God by being in a hurry to serve Him. One can be so busy about good works that God gets pushed outside the circle, even to the point of praying in a manner that has been attributed to General Charles DeGaulle—"O Lord, trust me."

### If I Want Your Advice, I'll Ask for It

"When people offer a preacher criticism, he ought to thank them for it and not be a smart aleck and sarcastic and certainly never say, 'If I want your advice, I'll ask for it.' Many a preacher has crushed himself to death and broken himself in pieces on the stone of opposition because he had that attitude," admonishes Grey. During the fight to pass the Sunday closing laws, J. D. (Journalist Daring) wrote an article in his church bulletin, *Evangel,* entitled "Never on Sunday," in which he appealed for an observance of the Sabbath. An elderly lady in his congregation called his hand on his malapropism. She wrote: "Dear Pastor: I notice in *The Evangel* this week that you have used 'Never On Sunday' as a quote. I don't believe you know the air given that expression. In the picture, 'Never On Sunday,' the story is about the life of a prostitute who worked at her trade diligently for six days but declined on the seventh, on Sunday. I fear more of our young people will also recognize the expression." Needless to say, the minister penned a warm note of thanks to his critic.

Early in his ministry he listened to a helpful critic about the use of humor. In 1938, J. D. was honored by Union University with a D.D. degree. At that time he was the youngest man ever to receive this honor and the man who had been out of school the fewest years. The evening before the awards ceremony J. D. spoke to an alumni banquet in which he used some of the humor which has been his forte. Dr. John Jeter Hurt, Sr., who had been pastor of First Baptist Church, Jackson, Tennessee, when J. D. was a student, and president of Union when J. D. was "doctored," wrote a note: "J. D., you have a great gift for the use of humor and sarcasm. You use it well, but always regard it. Do not use humor just for humor's sake; do not have sarcasm to the point of destruction; use them only when they get over a point and when they can help you to put across a message and help you to influence people."

Sometimes a man can be saved from unconscious error by listening to an observant critic. One of the poems Grey has used with great frequency at funerals and in sermons dealing with death is William Cullen Bryant's "To A Waterfowl." For years J. D. quoted the closing lines of the poem as follows:

> He who from zone to zone guides through the boundless sky
> Thy uncertain flight, and the long path I must tread
> Will guide my steps aright.

One of the men in the congregation said, "Pastor, I think if you will look it up, you'll find he said, 'Thy certain flight.' "

"Is that so?" J. D. responded. "I had the impression it was 'uncertain'."

"Look it up."

The friend was right—"Guide through the boundless sky thy certain flight." Once again grateful Grey said thanks to a critic.

If you live in the midst of human beings, J. D. G. knows (as should all of us) that you are sure to be criticized. And if you are human you will not like it. No matter how much you may say you welcome criticism, what you generally mean is that you would welcome any other sort of criticism than the kind you receive.

Critics are not necessarily infallible in their judgments of conduct   J. D. is a master of riposte when critics overvalue their suggestions. A Baptist layman who sought to use his critical sword too sharply when in truth the blade might have been turned upon himself, received a stinging rebuke: "Now listen, I am going to do like Abraham Lincoln said once to a critic, 'If you don't quit telling lies on me, I am going to start telling the truth on you.' " Grey adds, "He had his silver and gold, but I had my brass." Parenthetically, they are now warm friends.

"One must take criticism," admonishes Grey, "without hysteria, hatred, or humiliation, but with humility, honesty, and humor. In short, follow the advice of him who said of his critics, 'They are the unpaid guardians of my soul'."

Whatever the circumstances, a man cannot carry the burden of a grudge. J. D. was accused by a friend of being too generous toward people who would stab him in the back. His reason follows: "My heart isn't big enough to carry a grudge against people. And God is my witness, right this day, I say in all sincerity, that there is not a living person in this world that I carry a grudge against or sharpen my axe for. There are a lot of them I don't particularly care about and I don't seek out their company; nor do I hold a popularity contest for them, but I don't carry hatreds and animosities even against people who have done me wrong, you know."

Grey is unlike the Irish chaplain who hated the British. In every sermon he managed to strike a blow at the British. One day the post commander stopped him and said, "As long as I am in command, I do not want to hear another utterance from your lips that is critical of the British." Several months went by; then the chaplain could restrain himself no longer.

In the observance of the Lord's Supper he stated: "Jesus said, 'One of you will betray me'." Then the chaplain had Judas reply with a clipped British accent: "I say, ole chap, is it I?"

The Saint's files are pregnant with undelivered lectures, one being "Don't Be a Hired Man." Serious Grey states that no preacher should have the same feelings as the man described in Robert Frost's poem "The Death of the Hired Man": "He had nothing to look back on with pride and nothing to look forward to with hope." [5] "The minister is not a hired man," pleads J. D. "For as long as history has recorded it, important people have tried to purchase the voice of the preacher. The Scottish lords had the custom of appointing the pastors and controlling them. The Church of Scotland struggled long and hard before this ecclesiastical slavery chained by monthly stipends was abolished and the preachers were emancipated. Although the attitude may be rare, there are, even in the average congregation, people who let it be known in subtle ways that they pay for the preacher's chicken." Preacher Grey decries the attitude of too many members who look on the pastor as "Our man on Sunday," and agrees with a fellow Southern Baptist pastor who has stated emphatically, "Any church may fire me, but no church can hire me!"

In Grey humor he retells the story which was relayed to him by a former Southern Baptist Convention president, Brooks Hays. Mr. Hays' father, encountering a deacon friend on the square of an Arkansas town, asked in the course of their conversation about the health of the church. With some emotion, the rural brother answered, "Strange that you would ask! Our preacher ran off with all the money in our church treasury, $200." A bit alarmed, Mr. Hays inquired further, "Did you find him and did he have the money?"

Victoriously the deacon crowed, "You can bet your mule we found him. He didn't have the money, but we are going to make him preach out every dime of it!" Will the deacons please come forward to receive the offering!

The words of Carlyle Marney ring true to J. D.: "The Church has disguised itself from Him, and in order to keep Him away hires pastors, of whom its members frequently make *beggars*, to finance our own little kingdom; or *gigolos*, to charm our society friends in voice and manner when they come around to see God occasionally; or even *slave drivers*, if by chance we are big enough and the people are little enough; *sharecropper* tenants, here for a little while to tend crops not our own until the will of the owner sends us to other fields not our own; or, more frequently, we let them make us *plumbers*, suction pump in hand, unclogging stopped channels of grace all the ministry long, so elated when after months of effort some 'believer' begins to act like what he said he was years before; or glorified *glass blowers*, busy with bellows, and fire and glass, and breath, blowing our collapsed religion back into color and shape again; or better, in dodging Him we have made our spiritual leaders to be *bellwethers*, by which I mean that as pastor I am quite frequently expected to be a sexless sort of old goat who by ringing bells and bleating leads the sheep into the right pen for the slaughter '*in nomine Domini Jesu Christi*' and in the name of *religion*." [6]

J. D. forms Grey shadows on his brow in denouncing role-playing. To him many ministers are burdened with anxiety and guilt because of their inability to play the part of the supernatural, holy saint expected of them by the congregation. Morris Bishop caught the spirit in his poem, *The Perforated Spirit*.

The fellows up in Personnel,
They have a set of cards on me.
The sprinkled perforations tell
My individuality.
And what am I? I am a chart.
Upon the cards of IBM
The secret places of the heart.

It matters not how I may prate;
They punch with punishments my scroll.
The files are masters of my fate;
They are the captains of my soul.

Monday my brain began to buzz;
I was in agony all night;
I found out what the trouble was;
They had my paper clip too tight.[7]

One big reason Grey implores preachers not to allow themselves to be hired is because the hired man is never entrusted with tasks which require change. He only follows the job description. He is the assistant to the chaplain of the revered institution, Status Quo. He is the cleanup man who functions by sweeping halls, emptying cuspidors, picking up old funeral parlor hand fans in the hallowed ivy halls of Decrepit Academy, which, like all venerable institutions, has a Latin motto across its front: *Status Quo Ante*. Someone has defined *status quo* as "a herd of sacred cows grazing in a lush green pasture, and the more the herd multiplies the thinner the grass becomes." The seven last words of a church may come as a new revelation to some, but they are: "We never did it that way before "

Let the words of Dean Inge be heard clearly, "If a man marries the spirit of his generation, he will be a widower in the next." When one turns up the hearing aid to the judgments of Langdon Gilkey, the message is unmistakable:

"Protestantism should seek in our day to recapture its older tradition: that the pulpit, he who stands in it, and so the church as a whole, are first of all servants of the Word, not of the mind of the congregation."

Grey concludes, "Let us honor the past and take from it its fires but not its ashes, and move with confidence that God is still leading his people into great new revelations and into significant areas of service." The words of a motto on the wall of a Protestant monastery in France offer the meaningful admonition: "Do not be afraid to precede the dawn." As one has said: "We have loved the stars too fondly to be fearful of the night."

Lecture number two in the undelivered series might be entitled, *You are Not Top Sacred or Judgment-Proof*, in which Grey quotes a maxim of Roland Q. Leavell, "Allow every man a fault, because we have our own." He shares the personal conviction: "We all have our feet of clay—all of us do." The fact does not, in his opinion, warrant character assassination. "I want to get it on record, he says, "that anyone gossiped about needs a hearing whether the subject be a minister or anyone else. I will tell the young preacher who goes to a new church, 'You want to watch the fellow who comes up and begins to tell you all that was wrong with the last pastor. Mark it down—you are the next victim.'

"We all need much encouragement, particularly the fellow for whom others are gunning. Let the accusers come to me with your facts—then I will listen." We preachers ourselves are sometimes quick to judge one another without a hearing. The animal instinct grabs us as it does dogs when one is down in a fight, and all the others jump on him instead of standing up for him.

"In 1929, a Sunday school teacher wrote in the flyleaf of

my Bible a helpful verse I have used to encourage an injured brother:

> Men may misjudge thy aim,
> Think they have cause to blame,
> Say Thou art wrong.
> Go on thy quiet way.
> God is thy judge, not they,
> Fear not, Be Strong!"

In the ensuing years men, victims of criticism fall-out, whose backs have been used for target practice, have found strength in these oft-repeated words in brief penned notes from J. D. Since all holy men live under the gun of the compulsive critic, all share a standing invitation to join the company of the compassionate. "The Christian community in most of its glistening moments has always been able to take those who have suffered the worst shame, perversion, and depravity and lift them up to the highest heaven of hope and recovery." [8]

The Saint deplores the tragedy that some preachers have not learned the elementary lessons of professional ethics which are demonstrated consistently by groups of lawyers and doctors. "For the children of this world are in their generation wiser than the children of light" (Luke 16:8). Many preachers are so accustomed to shearing the sheep that they try it on a ram now and then. The habit of criticism is the hang-up of too many preachers. The flywheel on their mental mimeograph machines cannot turn fast enough to put out the new word on some unfortunate front runner. Nothing can temper the indignant wrath or dilute the unholy joy of the giant-killer like remembering, before pronouncing sentence, that no one is good enough nor knows enough nor loves enough to play God with his brother's reputation.

Grey warns the preacher to avoid the part played by cul-
prits reflected in the following parable of modern vintage:

A certain rising man was going up from anonymous vil-
lage to the city of acclaim, when he fell among the brethren,
who whispered away his coat of esteem, wounded him by
insinuation and departed, leaving his hopes and aspirations
only half alive. And by chance there happened by that way
the pastor's friend who knew quite well that the name of the
game is "Look on with great pity; pass on with great haste
and go tell it on the mountains—as soon as the WATS line
is clear." Likewise the ministerial scorekeeper came, and se-
curing identification and recording it in his black book, hur-
ried on to make the deadline for this year's book of reports.
But a certain "soul brother" as he journeyed came where he
was, and when he saw him had compassion on him. And he
went to him and bound up the wounds from the critics'
branding iron with the clean cloth of personal identification;
he poured on the hurt the healing oil of human understanding, carried the hurting one to his own house of recovery,
and made of his own house of reputation a recovery room for
the hurting one. . . . And he footed the bill for the dura-
tion. When the critics called to secure a progress report on
the patient, the soul brother met them with the steady eye of
responsibility, the indicting rumor that the patient would
live, and a plain statement to live with the consequences of
being a man for this other.

"The hottest brand going is not Conoco (gasoline)," smol-
ders Grey. It is the mark applied by reckless Pharisees walking about in sackcloth and ashes. *Your* sackcloth and *your*
ashes. The users of branding irons on men to identify them
as escaped slaves in the Roman period were neither as subtle, effective, or as quick as the modern users, who with a hot
hand and a cold heart, instead of mercy-killing a rumor,

breed it to a man-eating tiger and distribute its offspring with the same pleasant spirit as a child handing out extra puppies. They wouldn't dare be caught in a burlesque show, but when the ministerial striptease begins and one fellow begins to disrobe the dark and secret and tragic past of another, like juveniles next to the theatre runway they scream: "Take it off! Take it all off!" Their chanting builds up until it becomes a truly religious "Crucify him!"—with rusty nails —no dipping them in tetanus serum! They, the branders, become the little foxes who destroy the vines. Too many have felt panic like that of a fleeing criminal when brethren gave the full-throated chase like bloodhounds in hot pursuit. The American jury system is more lenient and justice—not "Lynch first—Trial will be held at leisure—Verdict unimportant!" The victim rides like Lady Godiva through the hostile stares of the peeping Toms—only he has been shorn of all protective cover. Who knows what evil lurks in the hearts of men? The Grey shadow knows . . . as does Brother Tom and Brother Dick and Brother Harry, and everybody else in the association knows in part.

Kentucky Baptist editor C. R. Daley adds fuel to the Grey fires, "Of all people who ought to be helpful to each other, it's preachers. The truth is, however, that preachers often are more thoughtless of one another than men of any other calling. Part of it is unintentional, but some of it is downright demonic.

There is no rule book or written code of ethics for Baptist pastors. There are, however, standards of conduct and rules of behavior which are generally understood. "Since there are no laws governing a pastor's conduct and no ethics committees to deal with him, he must be doubly careful to act discreetly in every instance. It is assumed every preacher is a Christian and a gentleman, and if he always acts accord-

ingly, his ministerial ethics will never pose any serious problems for his brothers in the ministry." [9]

"Fasten your seat belt," warns Grey. "Buckle up for
safety. The bread you cast on the water comes back."

*"Finally, Brethren . . ."*

In the privacy of his study, Grey warns, "Beware of little
old ladies of both sexes in and out of the church and, in the
words of the colorful P. H. Anderson, missionary to China,
'Watch with great diligence the preacher who says, Now,
Brethren, I say this in the spirit of love, for he is getting
ready to stab somebody'."

The third of undelivered lectures would be entitled *Don't
Be Afraid To Deal With the Issues.* Gordon Clinard, former
professor of preaching and fellow Union University alum-
nus of the Saint scores the advice of the retired pastor "who
attributed his success in the ministry to the fact that in
forty years of his pastorate, he had never preached on a controversial subject. Perhaps he was afraid of the situation
which had developed for a preacher in a cartoon. Looking
out over the four or five who interrupted the emptiness in
the church, he said, "So, I have decided to preach on a less
controversial subject."

For his motivation in dealing with the issues, Grey needs
only to turn to the Word, for it says, "To everything there is
a season and a time to every purpose under the heaven. A
time to be born and a time to die; a time to plant and a time
to pluck up; a time to weep and a time to laugh; a time to
keep and a time to cast away; a time to speak and a time to
keep silence . . ." (Ecc. 3:1-7). The problem is that too
many suffer from logorrhea when confronted by trivia; but
are struck dumb when it is time to speak to vital issues. "It
is easy to explain mistakes, for all honest men will under-

stand and sympathize; it is impossible to explain silence, for none will listen."

While science has long since welded this world into a neighborhood, Minister Grey muses that the church continues to drag in the effort to make it a brotherhood. The words of the new beat-generation song "Who Will Answer?" haunt men in their muteness. Christians, according to our preacher, are still playing the word game of the lawyer in Jesus' day. "Who is my neighbor?" When, indeed, one answers the questions "Who am I? Why am I?"—which of necessity requires biblical revelation?

Of all the ghosts rising out of the murky swamps of crisis none has haunted mankind with more nagging insistence than the dark issue of race. Situations and circumstances are complicated by background, training, and plaguing guilts. At best Christian efforts have been feeble lights to chase away the ghosts. J. D. (Justice Declaring) has been a wielder of the torch. With twenty-seven other leaders in the year 1956, he voiced an appeal for a Christian spirit in race relations. When silence opened the parlor door to extremists, he helped to formulate the following statement:

AN APPEAL . . . FOR A CHRISTIAN SPIRIT IN RACE RELATIONS

Southern Baptists and Negro Baptists constitute the largest Christian groups in the South. The consequences of failure to find a Christian solution to the problems of tension in race relations will rest more heavily upon these groups than others. In view of the many influences that are contributing to an emotional approach to these problems, it becomes urgently imperative that Christians consider them calmly and on the basis of Christian teachings.

In response to a request from the Advisory Council for Work with Negroes—a group of workers serving with various agencies in Southern Baptist life—we have been given the opportunity to express our personal convictions about this matter.

We are speaking as individuals, desiring to witness for Christ, and have no thought of speaking for Southern Baptists or for any church or agency affiliated with the Southern Baptist Convention.

We appeal to our Baptist brethren, white and Negro, and to other Christian friends, to give careful consideration to the following statement of principles, setting forth, we believe, the truth of the Bible and offered in the spirit of goodwill and Christian love:

God created man in his own image. Therefore, every man possesses infinite worth and should be treated with respect as a person.

Christ died for all men. Therefore, the Christian view of man, every man, must reflect the spirit of the cross.

God is no respecter of persons. Therefore, prejudice against persons or mistreatment of persons on the grounds of race is contrary to the will of God.

Christ said, "Thou shalt love thy neighbor as thyself." Therefore, Christians are obligated to manifest active good will toward all people and to help them to achieve their fullest potentialities as persons.

Christian love, as exemplified by Christ, is the supreme law for all human relations. Therefore, Christians have the assurance that such love, conscientiously practiced, will resolve tensions and bring harmony and good will in race relations.

Men whose minds and hearts shut the doors of communication and fasten them with the padlocks of prejudice do not readily admit even the dictums of Christ where race relations are concerned. Thereto we might ponder the influence of the foregoing statement. Channing Tobias would have interpolated or added as a postscript:

If you discriminate against me because I am dirty,
    I can make myself clean.
If you discriminate against me because I am bad,
    I can reform and be good.
If you discriminate against me because I am ignorant,
    I can learn.

If you discriminate against me because I am ill-mannered,
I can improve my manners.
But, if you discriminate against me because of my color,
You discriminate against me because of something God him-
self gave me and over which I have no control.

Grey proclaims that, if men spend too much time trying
to gain "things" from natural blessings and draw a circle
around themselves because of their greed and disinterest in
others, they are likely to find that all they have is "a sack of
garbage." In a real-life story, J. D. illustrates how some stal-
wart Christians may be called upon to infuse more of the
spirit of Christ into current life or consent to the demise of
righteousness in the land because of ugly intemperance:

It happened in Chicago. A bishop went out one night to address
a group of haters. They numbered warmongers and haters of
religion and races other than theirs. The bishop carried his word
of God to the group. There was a hushed silence as he walked out
of the hall—bottled-up stillness. Then a woman rose and began screaming: "Negro lover . . . Jew lover!!! Bishop, they call
you. It's Rabbi, you are." Then the woman spat on the face of the
bishop. In that crowd, with the feeling of murder in the hearts
of some of the men present, the bishop made no move to wipe his
cheek. Instead he turned the other cheek to face her. She was
overcome. Her voice was racked with sobbing and pleas for a
greater mercy. The bishop spoke again, simply: "Rabbi? That's
what they called my Lord."

Conversing at a late evening hour in the study of the
Saint, we agreed that "the Christian church and Christians
are on trial before the generations of the unborn. A hundred
years from now enlightened men will be asking, 'What was
the church thinking and saying while the air was being
poisoned for all mankind? What kind of preaching did it demand of its preachers? With what kind was it satisfied? Was

it satisfied with 'peace of mind' while the future was in total
jeopardy?

"The answer to such questions is being written at this moment, and we are the authors of that answer."

Conservative Grey adds a poignant addendum to his timely
"lectures," and he rumbles: "My innards just boil when I
think of some of the current trends which divide Southern
Baptists into camps of liberalism and conservatism and get
a feud going between the two. I do not agree with some of the
brethren, and I will dissent with them at every chance in
speeches or in private. But I don't buy the idea that you have
to be on my bandwagon in everything, agree with me on
everything, and measure your life in my little half-pint meas-
ures before I will even speak to you. I think men are doing a
great disservice to the denomination with their eternal tilt-
ing at windmills and stabbing straw men. Now I believe,
of course, in calling serious defectors to taw. But, I believe
in the boards of responsible agencies dealing with such men;
to make such things a convention-wide platform matter, I
don't believe in it!"

NEW  ORLEANS

ON

HIS  HEART

*I can think of New Orleans with only deep affection. I am glad I came here. I have hundreds of friends here in all walks of life and all faiths.*

J. D. Grey

*The city is proud of the leadership given by Dr. Grey. He has been active not only in church work, but in health, welfare, recreational and other activities. And he has been outspoken when this was needed. When others have climbed into their shells, Dr. Grey has spoken his mind. And that's good for a community. I thank him in behalf of our city.*

City Councilman James E. Fitzmorris, Jr.

*If you can meet with Triumph and Disaster*
*And treat those two impostors just the same.*

## SHADES ABOUT GREY

The New Testament records that even in the early "good ole days" there were preachers who asked to be invited out to broader pastures and more compatible circumstances. Perhaps the pastorium in Crete had begun to leak or the deacons had turned down the pastor's latest idea for packing the pew; for Timothy wanted out, and who could write a better letter of recommendation than Uncle Paul. Paul's answer was a terse, "For this cause left I thee in Crete."

"Now Crete was a hell-hole if there ever was one," and in this parallel situation J. D.'s implication is that New Orleans had been considered a graveyard for evangelical witness. "When I had been here just a few years Will Henry Knight had a revival. One morning after the service he said, 'J. D., let's drive around a little.' As we had planned to eat with some men downtown, we had time for a drive through Audubon Park. I never shall forget—I like to date things and incidents—as we turned off St. Charles Avenue to go into Audubon Park, Knight said, 'J. D., how long have you been here?' I told him perhaps five or six years. He said, 'Well I always believed if a man stays at a place seven years he can stay there as long as he wants to.'

"I have said about New Orleans, frequently and even recently, that is the type of town that first gets on your nerves; next in your hair (or maybe it gets in your hair first, then on your nerves); and finally on your heart. Then you're stuck!

"It was an excruciating, agonizing experience when I moved here from Denton, Texas. In Denton, for example, if something went wrong with our plumbing, I'd call up a guy and say, 'Bill (Langford there in my church was a plumber), our plumbing is out of order. Could you come over and fix it?' 'Sure, sure, Brother Grey (or J. D.) be right over.' He'd be there in thirty minutes. In New Orleans, I could call a guy and he would say, 'Well, we can get there next Tuesday.' Maybe next Tuesday he wouldn't show up or even call. I would experience the same frustration with car repair. In Denton I'd stand around while the mechanic would get in my car and say, 'This is what's wrong, Brother Grey. It'll take me a couple of hours to fix it if you'll wait, or you may come back and get it.' Now in the city when I take my car for repair, it's like checking a patient into the hospital. A man in a long white coat downstairs, after writing up the ticket and case history on the car, says, 'Well, we can give it to you late tomorrow evening.' The contrast between the slow-moving service in the large city and the quick personal attention in the small town gets on my nerves, but the Antique Lady on the Mississippi has gotten on my heart and I'm stuck with her."

Salutes and tributes concerning the Grey one rise out of newspaper files like Christian bodies out of graveyards on Resurrection Day. Notable among these is a quotation from the introduction of J. D. Grey to the meeting of the Missouri pastors by Walter Pope Binns, President of William Jewell College in June, 1961.

"Dr. Grey is pastor of the great First Baptist Church of New Orleans. There was a time when New Orleans was the graveyard of Baptist preachers because the Baptists were few in number and were so overshadowed in that Catholic city. The Baptist situation has taken on a new aspect in recent years, and the situation is entirely changed. In seeking the cause for this change we naturally think of the powerful influence of the New Orleans Baptist Seminary and the Southern Baptist Hospital. It is true that these institutions have made a significant contribution, but the President of Tulane University told me that among all the men of the past or present, living or dead, Dr. J. D. Grey had exerted the greatest influence in bringing about this change in New Orleans. As pastor of the First Baptist Church and as a citizen of New Orleans he has projected his personality and exerted his leadership which has changed the Baptist image and influence throughout the city."

The *Times Picayune* stated editorially: "Dr. Grey has provided spiritual leadership and inspiration to New Orleans' largest Protestant congregation. And together, Dr. Grey and his church have played significant roles in every project of civic betterment through the years.

"Dr. Grey is a man of exceptional qualities. And all of his splendid attributes of intellect, integrity, courage, and compassion he has devoted unstintingly to his church and his community. His influence has been widespread.

"It is with a deep sense of gratitude that this city joins Dr. Grey's congregation in recognition of his continuing contribution to our spiritual and civic well being."

"Dr. J. D. Grey Wins Shining Laurels" by Paul Kalman, New Orleans *Item:* "Those who know Dr. Grey and who have worked with him registered no surprise when they received word of his election to the Louisiana Baptist Convention presidency. By watching and analyzing his vibrant, dynamic personality, they have learned that J. D. Grey takes two steps at a time when he is climbing the ladder of success.

"People gifted with super-abundance of ambition are some-times easily blinded by their achievements. As a result, they build around themselves a wall of impregnability to the advice of their neighbors.

"Dr. Grey said he has never let himself forget that when fortune smiles upon a man, she is doing so only because it is the will of God so to benefit a man who has devoted his life and career to His service.

"The net result of his unusual combination of forcefulness and kindliness is that Dr. Grey has a reputation of being one of the most popular ministers ever to set foot in or out of New Orleans. Everywhere he goes he makes friends of the people who hear and meet him. He is constantly sought after to speak at civic and social affairs as well as churches."

Pope Paschall's only living grandson, Dr. H. Franklin Paschall, then president of the Southern Baptist Convention, speaking *ex cathedra*, of course, stated: "I count it a high privilege to pay tribute to a man I have loved and honored through all my ministerial life. I have appreciated the ecumenical character of the meeting tonight, Dr. Grey. And it may be appropriate for me to remind some if they do not know that there was a Pope once by the name of Paschall. He was the sorriest Pope in the history of the Roman Catholic Church, and that may be the reason I am a Baptist. I even delighted in that greeting from Governor Lurline Wallace by George!

"Pastor of the First Baptist Church for 30 years! My hat goes off to any man who can be pastor of any Baptist church for 30 years (especially in New Orleans). I followed a man in Nashville, Tennessee, who had been pastor of that church for 34 years, Dr. W. F. Powell. You knew him well, Dr. Grey. And in some respects these two men are alike—both of them big operators; both of them very popular; top flight public relations men. Dr. Powell was chaplain because they wanted him to be able to break the speed limit legally.

"One day Dr. Powell was going from Nashville to Lebanon, which is 30 miles from Nashville, and the highway patrolman took out after him. Finally he pulled him over on the side of the road and said, 'Dr. Powell, I know you are a man of God. I know the Lord has taken care of you. But you can have a wreck. I don't mind your breaking the speed limit, but you passed me and I was chasing somebody.' I will not press the parallel. I just think there is a similarity between these two notable characters."

The Grey streak is a man in a hurry but with deliberate speed. He learned early that breakneck speeds usually precipitate pileups short of the finish line. He remembers the west Texas boy, Elmer by name, who was reputed to be able to outrun anything that came his way.

One day an oilman in a brand new Lincoln Continental slid through the dust into the gas station—grocery store owned by Elmer's father. Raising the hood and seeing the motor, the man said, "Man, what a motor! My son Elmer sure would like to race you!" The oilman inquired, "What kind of car does your son have?" "He don't have no car; he'll just flat outrun you." With a note of intrigue the Lincoln owner asked, "Where is he?" A shout brought Elmer rambling out, in overalls and tennis shoes, to the front of the station. With disbelief the oilman found himself lining up and hearing the roar of an ancient six-gun signal the start. Tearing across the West Texas desert, he watched his speedometer climb and, incredibly, Elmer stayed beside him.

Putting his foot all the way through the floorboard, he suddenly was aware of wind and debris in the air. He didn't look back, but roared on across the finish line. Elmer was nowhere in sight. Slowly the driver wheeled back along the course—and found Elmer stacked up in a ditch—a mass of cuts, bruises, and abrasions. "Elmer, are you hurt? What stopped you? Did you trip and fall?" "Naw," drawled Elmer. "Mister, have you ever had a tennis shoe blow out at a hundred and twenty miles an hour?!"

Paschall continued: "If I were giving my remarks a title, perhaps it should be 'Dr. J. D. Grey, A Committed Man'— committed first and always to our Lord Jesus Christ. Growing out of this commitment and as a result of it, he is a great churchman, a responsible citizen, an inspiring and dynamic leader. When I was a student at Union University, I began to hear this man speak. His achievements were topics of conversation on our campus, in our conferences, and at our conventions. So I have looked toward this man for more than twenty-five years with admiration and appreciation and affection. And to have the honor of being here tonight to say these few words is just about the best thing that could happen to me. He delivered our baccalaureate address or sermon when I graduated in 1944. I do not remember all that he said. I do not remember the subject that he used. But I do remember that he said he'd just as soon go to heaven from New Orleans as from any place in the world. So you see that far back he had a dedication to this community as well as to this church which has made possible the achievements that we recognize tonight."

From closer home, too close for comfort for some, come the warm words of W. Lawrence Chapman, then chairman of the deacons of First Baptist Church.

As you have looked over the program tonight and see all of these dignitaries taking part, I am sure you would agree that there is no use for someone like me coming up here to try to say anything. As the Mayor said, "It is hard to say anything following all of these distinguished guests and speakers." But when I get down

here and I have to follow something like you just heard from
Billy Graham and Norman Treigle, I am really squeezed in between something, if you know what I mean. Then I look down
here and I see "Thirty Years of Progress—W. Lawrence Chapman." That's for me. Actually I guess the progress is that it took
me thirty years to be chairman of the deacons here. But if I were
to say something that I wanted to say about what this thirty
years of progress really means, in so far as this charming couple
that we are honoring tonight, I would have to say that it is
togetherness.

Thirty years ago when J. D. and Lillian Grey came here through
God's calling and brought us together, those of us who were here
wondered what Dr. Grey would say first. Well, we are still won-
dering what he will do next. We don't know what he did first. Actually I can't remember. But you can be sure, whatever he does,
he is promoting goodwill toward his fellow man. In fact, his entire
attitude is to promote.

He reminds me of the story of the two shoe salesmen who were
sent to Africa for their companies. One of them wired back,
"The case is hopeless. Nobody wears shoes." The other wired his
employer, "Unlimited opportunities. Everybody barefooted."

J. D. Grey is also always seeking the opportunity to do good.
The old adage, "Life however short is made still shorter by waste
of time," surely would indicate a long life for J. D. and Lillian
Grey, because both of them stay too busy to waste any time. Like
our celebration tonight, that day in '37 when they came to New
Orleans was also an important date for the First Baptist Church.
We know as the prophet Amos said, "Two cannot walk together
except they be agreed." Well, we have agreed on almost everything, but sometimes we have had to compromise. Dr. Grey is
somewhat like my wife as far as that compromising goes. When
my wife and I disagree, we compromise. I do what she says. The
membership of the First Baptist Church hasn't necessarily agreed
with everything Dr. Grey has said, but our record is indicative
of his strong leadership. Together we have had some very reward-
ing experiences. Together, as pastor and people, God has blessed
us.

As James L. Sullivan said during the dedication of the
Baptist Book Store on the campus of New Orleans Baptist
Theological Seminary in 1967: "I have heard many people
in the Southern Baptist Convention say there are three in-
stitutions responsible for the growth of Baptists in New
Orleans—the Seminary, Southern Baptist Hospital, and
J. D. Grey."

From the heart of a grateful public servant, Honorable
Victor H. Schiro, Mayor of the City of New Orleans, on
J. D.'s thirtieth anniversary:

It is quite unusual, of course, to have a pastor with a church for
as long as thirty years. But I guess you wanted him so badly, and
you have held on to him so tightly, that he is here with us, and I
hope he will be here for the rest of his life. Dr. Grey is a man of
great community spirit. Whenever we call on him for anything,
whatever it is, he is always willing to serve his city in any ca-
pacity, to be of service. I know him well, believe me. I have
worked with him a great deal. And I have two things here—one
that I prepared specially, I want you to know, for Dr. Grey. It
is this: New Orleans has always been fortunate in the character
and quality of its people. This has been particularly true of its
leaders. And I suggest that among the many people that I have
known, you tower high, not only in my esteem, but in the admiration and respect of the community at large. Thus it is a singular
privilege for me to herewith testify officially and personally, that
you, sir, are truly a man of spirit, dedication, and excellence. In
simple words, a complete citizen. I'd like to present this to you,
Dr. Grey.

In behalf of your city government I'd also like to present to you
a well-earned merit, a certificate of merit from your city which
says, "Be it known that for outstanding service, the city of New
Orleans has conferred the Certificate of Merit upon Dr. J. D.
Grey" with our compliments, sir. And this little gold key with
our affection.

In Georgia a well-loved journalist preacher, Dr. Louis D.

Newton, captured the spirit of the saint in his *Christian Index* column: "The guest of Pastor J. D. Grey of the First Church, I was told by taximen, hotel porters, newsboys, and non-Baptist leaders that Dr. Grey is the most influential evangelical leader in New Orleans. Pastor of the historic First Church, constituted December 28, 1843, since 1937, Dr. Grey has not only led that great church to its present magnificent location and physical facilities, but throughout the community he has established both the Baptist and evangelical witness in a fashion to gladden the hearts of Christians everywhere. The story of New Orleans henceforth will certify the Grey saga."

From fellow humorist, the late F. B. Thorn, pastor of First Baptist Church, Wichita, Kansas, came a note: "Dear J. D.: Thanks a lot for your card which has the picture of your new church. Congratulations to you, just stay in there and pitch. Just last week I was telling some fellows that you really have taken New Orleans and gone with it. I think you know that you are the first Baptist that has ever dented that Catholic city. In my books no man in America has tackled as hard a job and done it so successfully under the power of God as you have done in New Orleans. You are my best illustration of what can be done under most difficult conditions.

"Do not know anything I would like better than to sit down with you and have about two hours discussing the low-down on the high-ups."

J. D. (Joining Daily) has not been a joiner of every organization, for this would have been a dissipation for even a man of his remarkable energies. He soon discovered that you cannot join everything that comes along. Recalling the woman who moved into a small town and was opening a bank account, the president of the bank greeted her, and during the conversation, inquired commercially, "Would you like to join the Christmas Club?" Eagerly she replied, "Oh, yes! When does it meet?"

On occasions the Saint has been heard to say, "I used to join everything that came along, shake hands six different ways and massage a man up to his elbow. But I have decided that if a man belongs to a Baptist church and is married to one woman, he has enough to keep any man busy." Nevertheless, New Orleans is on my heart. To paraphrase Robert Frost, 'I have a lover's quarrel with New Orleans, I am jealous for the old Crescent City'."

## Man About Town

Although he can be seen at the symphony and the opera in formal attire, his usual working uniform as a man about town does not include a high hat and tails. The cane is J. D.'s constant friend as he plays out his availability for worthy causes.

A page from his diary reads: "One of the biggest kicks my family got was some time back when the Louisiana Arthritis Foundation had a seminar up at the Jewish Community Center. They called on me to be moderator of that meeting. My doctor was there—an eminent rheumatologist, Dr. Thomas Weiss of the Foundation—plus other outstanding medical people and officials. I moderated the meeting, and had a ball. I told more funny stories. I mean I got them laughing, and the doctors said to me, 'You did more to help this meeting than we did because you made these poor sufferers— about 250 or 300 people there—you made them feel that to have arthritis isn't the end of the road. The fact that you walked in here with a cane and a stiff leg gave encouragement to them.' I had a dozen of them to come up to me after it was over to shake hands with me and thank me and say,

'Well, you gave me a new hope to go on in spite of it.' One wild thing I said, 'I want to quote a proverb, an old Arab proverb: "I complained that I had no shoes until I met a man who had no feet." ' I said, 'By George, come to think about it, isn't this a heck of a place to quote an Arab proverb!' And they roared—it was in the Jewish Center. Come to think of it, though, I think it was really a Persian proverb. Whoever said it, it had doggone good philosophy?

J. D.'s involvement in secular causes, so named, and his availability in charitable endeavors are always a bit surprising to those who are locked into small pastures. There is no inconsistency, for "one hand open in charity is better than two closed in prayer."

All of the worthwhile causes in the city, no matter what combination of the alphabet is on their letterhead or what religious initials describe their sponsors, have received the promoting skills of the man about town. Ferdinand V. Grayson, Executive Director of the United Fund, an eyewitness to the man who has covered the waterfront city and her people for thirty years observed:

It is a distinct pleasure to me to be representing the United Fund here tonight in honoring a real friend, J. D. Grey. For 30 years Dr. Grey has been a tower of strength and a leader in the United Fund movement and in the Community Chest, which preceded the United Fund. In the interest of those two minutes on the non-existent clock up there, I will not even attempt to enumerate the many specific activities and services performed by Dr. Grey on behalf of the United Fund and all of the agencies in the Fund. I am sure you know that it's the story of a man of God who has been dedicated and zealous in service to his fellow man and his community. I wanted to single out just one thing, however, specifically about Dr. Grey, and this has to do with the success of the United Fund Loaned Executive program which is now five years old. In this program business firms in the community have loaned to the United Fund for the months of September and October one or more of their personnel to backstop the 18,000 volunteers in this community-wide fund raising effort. The 40 loaned executives spend three days in orientation at the beginning of this program. Dr. Grey, by demand on the part of the loaned executives, has been our number one speaker in these orientation sessions. What he has done every year is to communicate to the loaned executives the importance of their efforts in spiritual tones. They catch the basic truth that they are serving God by serving people and building a better community through their efforts in the United Fund drive. Dr. Grey has been a source of inspiration, the result of which has really inspired these loaned executives to go forth, and it isn't entirely a coincidence that these last five United Fund drives have been over-the-top successes. So it is in this context that I now want to present Dr. Grey with something that I have learned is called technically "commemorative coins." This is a token of our appreciation and esteem in which we hold him. On one side it says, and by the way, this whole idea of this coin was inspired by our loaned executives who have come to know J. D. and love him, because they know he is a coin collector as I am sure you all know, and not only that, but he has shared his coins with us, and he has drawn many a lesson of stewardship among us in the United Fund by the use of these coins that he has used, and we carry them with us. So, it is in this context, therefore, that we have made the only one of its kind—it has the United Fund touch in it—and it said, "United Fund to J. D. Grey, May 9, 1967," and a Bible verse has so been inscribed, from Psalm 119:105. I am not going to ask you good Baptists what it is as a good Methodist or attempt to be a good Methodist. I didn't know what it was, and it does say, "Thy Word is a lamp to my feet and a light to my path." That's how they feel about J. D. Grey, and that's how I feel about him.

John Wesley is remembered as the man whose parish was the world. Great men have a way of slipping the chains that would enclose them in narrow alleys. If New Orleans is on J. D.'s heart, the world and its needs can claim no loss.

There are those who pretend to address the world as in

the case of the evangelist in Alabama who cranked up his daily appeal over a one-watt radio station shouting in his leather-lunged gasp, "Hello, World!" And there are those few in whom the world sees a knowing and answering spirit.

Around the globe, people whose residence precludes their being members of First Baptist Church are part of that larger congregation which is caught up in J. D.'s ministry. Norman Treigle, opera star, confides, "No matter where I go throughout the world, when someone asks, 'What church do you go to in New Orleans?' and I answer, 'First Baptist,' they will say, 'J. D. Grey's church.' That's somewhat like being half-way home."

The man in a hurry is not a dash man but a cross-country runner. He is a jetsetter whose vapor trails cross the skies to Baptist World Alliance meetings around the world and to speaking engagements in Virginia or California, Montana, or Mississippi. Like Robert Frost:

> The woods are lovely, dark and deep.
> But I have promises to keep
> And miles to go before I sleep.
> And miles to go before I sleep.[1]

# THE

# CONSERVATIVE ECUMANIAC

*I salute him as a man of the people whose love for all classes and all religious groups has distinguished his famous ministry.*

*I salute him as a man of faith. His faith is biblical and his expression of that faith is found in myriad patterns of human service. His ministry to his Baptist people endears him to our Baptist family, but his faith and love extend beyond denominational limits.*

Brooks Hays

*I have seen a spirit of understanding, tolerance, and respect develop among Catholic, Jew, and Protestant. There is no place in New Orleans or anywhere else for religious snobbery. In free America the three great faiths have grown to gigantic stature as nowhere else.*

J. D. Grey

*My dear friend, consider: I am not persuading you to leave or change your religion, but to follow after that fear and love of God without which all religion is vain. I say not a word to you about your opinions or outward manner of worship. But I say, all worship is an abomination to the Lord, unless you worship him in spirit and in truth, with your heart as well as your lips, with your spirit and with your understanding also. Be your form of worship what it will, but in everything give him thanks, else it is all but lost labor. Use whatever outward observances you please; but put your whole trust in him, but honor his holy name and his word, and serve him truly all the days of your life.*

Written by John Wesley in 1749
To a Catholic friend

# VIGNETTE 6

*If neither foes nor loving friends can hurt you,*
*If all men count with you, but none too much.*

## SHADES OF GREY

"I'm asking that the spiritual skyline keep up with the growth of the city's skyline. We must join in spirit with the other religious groups to lift up the moral tone of the nation."

J. D. (Jewish Diocesan) Grey thus reveals the essential spirit of the man who will not be happy locked into any narrow sectarian corral. The kind of city he wants in the kind of world he wants demands that all men of good link hearts in a chain of righteousness. Some have thought it bizarre that this born-and-bred-in-landmarkism Baptist would develop such lasting and deep working friendships with men of so diverse denominational and theological shades as have been, and are, his associates. Nor has his own peculiar Baptistic autonomy been compromised an inch—iron-grey man that he is!

The subtle shades of Grey were painted in a striking spectrum of contrasts as he addressed the Southern Baptist Convention meeting in Miami Beach, Florida, in 1967. The following remarks are excerpts from that message:

## THE FELLOWSHIP OF KINDRED MINDS

With deep emotion and fervent spirit, we Baptists love to sing the grand old hymn "Blest Be the Tie That Binds," written by John Fawcett, the English Baptist preacher, in 1772. Our congregations sing it in their services. The annual meetings of many

District Baptist Associations are closed with it. Many State Conventions, just before the benediction of the last session, stand and sing with great feeling "Blest Be the Tie that Binds." And then in the annual sessions of this Southern Baptist Convention, thousands of messengers from the 50 states of our nation, mingle their voices in singing it. Our mighty Baptist World Alliance has virtually made it our "international anthem." In Christian love we shall continue to sing, "The fellowship of kindred minds is like to that above."

Now let us ask ourselves in all candor how "kindred" must our minds be in order for fellowship like to that above? Must there be a complete uniformity? Must we, before we can sing it, see eye to eye on every detail of life? If so, then it would be next to impossible for us to sing it in any Baptist gathering, including the local church. Furthermore, I doubt that any of us could sing it even as a solo, for precious few of us are in complete agreement with our own selves. Nevertheless, we as Baptists go on singing, "Blest be the tie that binds" in our various gatherings including the Baptist World Alliance because we are of "kindred minds" on the centrality of Christ and His Lordship over our lives.

Let us move on into another sphere and ask ourselves another question. This is a hard question that must be asked and answered in our most cultivated Christian conscience. The question is, How far am I as a Baptist willing to go in singing "Blest be the tie that binds" with other Christians who are not Baptists? This is a hard question that demands a direct answer in today's world. Each individual must search his own heart for the answer. We must examine our own "mandate to minister through Christian fellowship."

Ecumenism is a word being widely used today. It is used most inappropriately by many and is often understood the least by those who use it the most. To some it means just one thing: "organic union—a world church." In its derivation from the Greek it means "worldwide, universal." Basically it is not a bad word. It is made bad only by its misuse and improper application.

My dear Baptist brethren, I plead with you now that we shall all practice what we preach including this doctrine of cooperation.

Let us return briefly to the questions which we asked earlier— Can and will the Southern Baptist Convention become a part of the organizational structure of the ecumenical movements? We answer emphatically, "Yes—when." Yes, it can and will when the President of this Convention can tell the smallest one of our churches who must be its pastor. Yes, it can and will when Dr. Porter Routh and the Executive Committee can tell an autonomous local church how it must run its affairs. Baptists believe in the autonomy of the local church. Each church, therefore, when it expresses its own belief or policy expresses the belief of no other than its own members. These local churches of ours are in voluntary cooperation with the Southern Baptist Convention. This Convention has no business committing our 33,000 churches and 11 million members to affiliation in organizations and support of movement when they have no way of expressing their dissent except to withdraw from the Convention.

Thus far we have been looking at only one side of the coin—affiliation with ecumenical organizations. Let us now turn the coin over and look at the other side. And be assured, brethren, there is another side to the coin. This side has to do with Christian fellowship, brotherly love, and unity of the spirit, not union of organizations. Let us be just as frank, just as bold, and as full of sincere Christian conviction as we were in looking at the other side of the coin.

As Southern Baptists our image has often been marred by an exclusivism that has kept us in our local communities from being good neighbors and friends of other Christians, cooperating with them in worthy projects upon which we agree. In years gone by when we were largely limited to parochial, county, and even state areas, we could practice exclusivism. However, in this space age this is a luxury we can ill afford. We can no longer be little isolated islands in the great ocean of mankind. We cannot, we must not, draw our pharisaical robes about us and remain aloof from other Christians and men of goodwill.

I became pastor of the First Baptist Church, New Orleans, on May 1, 1937. Soon after my arrival I came to realize that our 27 churches of the New Orleans Baptist Association, with only 8,308 members, must cooperate with other denominations in civic and community projects aimed at building a better city. I realized we could not "go it alone" and accomplish very much. As chairman of the Social Betterment Committee of our Protestant Ministerial Union, I saw the members of that union, almost to a man, become vocal in a fight against gambling, crime, and corruption in government. Unitedly we went to the public and aroused its conscience. Business leaders took up the challenge and changes• have come. New Orlean's isn't perfect. But when you come there in 1969 for the Southern Baptist Convention you will see a city of 1,060,000 that is vastly different from what it was when the Convention last met there in 1937. Christians working together have been able to do more, much more, than we Baptists could have ever done working alone.

In that crusade our committee called on Archbishop Rummel at the Chancellery of the Roman Catholic Archdiocese of New Orleans. He received us cordially. For nearly three hours we discussed with him and his aides the shameful situation then current. It would not be proper for me to divulge the details of that conference. Suffice it to say that soon thereafter a letter from the Archbishop was read in every church in the Archdiocese condemning gambling, vice, and corruption.

I have seen this blessed "doctrine of cooperation" bring success in many worthy endeavors these 30 years. We have taken a religious census of the metropolitan area twice and each time with the cooperation of the Archdiocese. A few years ago something was seen in New Orleans which I doubt any other city has ever seen. An effort was being made to induce our State Legislature to enact a workable Sunday closing law. The effort was successful. But the unique thing was that one day all over the area there appeared full-size billboards and full-page advertisements in the newspapers urging enactment of this Sunday closing law. These were signed by, among others, the Greater New Orleans Federation of Churches, the Louisiana Diocese of the Episcopal Church, the Archdiocese of the Catholic Church of New Orleans, and the New Orleans Baptist Association.

Brethren, we Southern Baptists have spearheaded many noble efforts through the years. We have asked for and have received wholehearted cooperation of our brethren in other denominations in temperance, law enforcement, separation of church and state, social justice, united efforts against corruption in government, and many other projects too numerous to mention. We simply cannot "go it alone." We need them, and they need us!

If you want to know what cooperation really does, talk to one of these noble missionaries who has served in a foreign land. He will tell you that when you and a little handful of fellow believers are dropped down in a pagan country, you begin to search for kindred minds, you begin to reach out for the hand of other Christians who acknowledge the lordship of Christ and that you will stand with your shoulders together and your backs to the wall facing the on-slaught of the pagan hordes. You then begin to realize that literally you either hang together or you will hang separately.

We Baptists through our long history have been the freest and the most understanding of other faiths. Believing strongly as we do in soul freedom and salvation by grace, we have never taught that one must be a Baptist to be saved.

We must do more than cooperate with fellow Christians of other churches. We must manifest Christian fellowship toward every person who accepts the lordship of Jesus Christ. Let us return for a brief moment to the "Truett Statement" approved by this Con-vention in Baltimore in 1940. Addressed to the World Council of Churches, it opened with the words, "Dear Brethren." And re-spectfully declining the invitation of the World Council of Churches, the last paragraph of the statement says: "In conclusion, permit us to express the sincere desire of our hearts that the followers of Christ may all be one, not necessarily in name and in a world organization, but in spiritual fellowship with the Father and the Son. If Christ dwells in all our hearts by faith, we shall be brought into a spiritual unity that cannot be broken. We invoke the blessings of the triune God upon all who name the name of our Lord Jesus Christ."

Beloved, if you will allow me to say so, I believe we need to be-gin anew to practice the fine art of Christian fellowship among ourselves as Baptists. We know we have never been able to see eye to eye with one another on everything. But we can disagree without being disagreeable. Let us seek always to be Christians in our relations with each other. Let us strive to always show Christian courtesy, patience, kindness, and understanding.

He [Truett] offered several splendid suggestions concerning

what the Alliance can do in promoting understanding and cooperation among members of our Baptist family in the world. Among
other things he said, "We must avoid rash or studied generaliza-
tions in regard to other member bodies in the Baptist World
Alliance and relinquish denunciation as a substitute for reconciliation. We must face and discuss frankly differences of views or
traditions in fraternal forums rather than in headlines which encourage controversy and impute unchristian motives."

My beloved brethren, we Southern Baptists do have a mandate
and I believe it is from God, to minister through Christian fellowship. We have a responsibility to discharge.

The theme of EXPO '67 was suggested by a terse statement
contained in a book entitled, *Man and His World*, by the eminent
French author Antoine de Saint-Exupéry. That statement is: "To
be a man is to feel that by setting one's stone in place, one can
contribute to building the edifice of the world."

We Southern Baptists have a stone to set in place in building
the Kingdom of Christ. Let us do it as we sing:

> Blest be the tie that binds
> Our hearts in Christian love;
> The fellowship of kindred minds
> Is like to that above.

## In Scope

The Conservative Ecumaniac has drawn tribute from expected and unexpected sources alike. A fellow pastor states:
"The New Orleans Story has been told throughout our Southern Baptist Convention and, yet, this inspiring drama of
Baptist growth and development in New Orleans is incom-
plete without an acknowledgement of our 'Baptist diplomat.' . . . The people of New Orleans—the Catholics, the
Protestants, the white and the colored—love and respect Dr.
Grey. He has not confined his interests to his own large and
growing pastorate but has kept his hand and heart on the
pulse-beat of 'America's Most Interesting City.'. . . Because

of Dr. Grey's diplomacy, it has given me—as well as other Baptist ministers—a much better status in the eyes of this community."

On J. D.'s thirtieth anniversary at First Baptist Church, Julian B. Feibelman, Rabbi of Temple Sinai, who preceded the Saint into New Orleans by a mere three weeks, said:

Mr. Chairman, I shall take my cue from you and be very brief. The clock up there still points to midnight, and when the hand gets to two minutes past I shall sit down. I want to bring the Chairman also up to date on his biblical sport report. He failed to mention that Eve stole first and Adam stole second. And that Abel was struck out and Cain walked. Noah had to call the game off on account of rain, and poor Moses got such a headache that God had to give him two tablets. Dr. and Mrs. Grey, this is a very great honor to be able to participate in this tribute to you tonight for your 30 years as Pastor of First Baptist Church in New Orleans. I remember when you came here, you were not nearly as big a man; your church wasn't nearly as large. It was this little church on Delachaise and St. Charles. When I see this great establishment here, comprising practically an entire city block, I wonder how in the world he did it. I suppose the best way to explain it is the story they tell of a rabbi who was known somewhat for his sensational sermon topics and he announced one Friday night that he was going to speak on the following Friday night on the subject of Sex Appeal. One old lady nudged her neighbor in the second row and said, "Every week he has got to make another appeal." Maybe that's the way he did it.

I was asked to be very brief tonight, and I suppose it is all right for Baptist ministers to be brief, but it's not good form for a rabbi. He is expected to talk at length. I know you are awaiting the principal speaker tonight. I think it's a wonderful tribute to Dr. Grey to have brought a paschal lamb to be sacrificed in his name. Well, the clock hasn't moved yet. My two minutes haven't even begun. I mentioned before it was a great honor to be here and it is. I am very proud of the fact that I can participate with you tonight honoring this wonderful pastor and minister. I could say a great many things about him that are good, but I was told beforehand by the committee that everybody is going to say something good about him, and I should say a few things that were not so good, because the program is going to get better as it goes along. But I can't really think of anything that isn't good to say about him. He has been a wonderful public spirit. He has participated in things not only here in New Orleans and in Louisiana and for his own people, but he has represented our government. He has received plaudits and acclaim here and there and on the four corners of the earth. It must be a wonderful feeling for you, J. D., to have reached this period in your life still able, alert, still strong, and still growing, and with a wonderful group to work with. And I congratulate you on it, and all you have achieved.

I think we are all now at the verge of a new era in our religious work, and that is the spirit by which we may all come together in this wonderful and lovely fashion as tonight to pay to one another our respects and our honor in this spirit that has pervaded this city for a number of years now. It is called the ecumenical spirit. The beauty of this is that we can do this sincerely and genuinely without sacrificing one iota, or changing one jot or tittle of our own faith; having to compromise absolutely nothing; and yet opening our hearts to the teachings which all of our faiths give to us to love one another as brothers. I am thankful to God some of us have lived long enough to see that moment here and to enjoy it. I want to close by revealing to you one thing that you perhaps do not know—that's about your minister. This is a beautiful program tonight, printed magnificently, but not once do you see the name of your pastor—only the initials. Well, I think it's time for me to reveal what that name is: in the true ecumenical spirit, *Jewish Diocesan* Grey. I want, Dr. and Mrs. Grey, to apologize for the time I took, but it was in my heart to say these things. I thank you for the privilege. I ask God to bless you both and give you strength; in fact, as we say in the Talmud, that you may continue from strength to strength.

Another tribute on the occasion of Dr. Grey's thirtieth anniversary came from George H. Wilson, Executive Secretary of the Greater New Orleans Federation of Churches:

Wouldn't you like to follow this chairman or Dr. Feibelman?

Really, it's a rough assignment. I'm not too much surprised about this deacon who woke up in the middle of the service and said, "It's not my time to lead, I just dealt," because the other Sunday I heard two bookies leaving the First Baptist Church here in the city and one of them was saying to the other one, "It's hallelujah, stupid, not Hialeah."

Dr. Grey has been a marvelous friend of the Wilsons and the Federation of Churches ever since we have been in the city, and it has been my privilege to spend almost half of that 30 years in the city with him and with you. I have looked upon him as an advisor and as a father confessor. As a matter of fact, there have been times when I have felt like calling him Father, but he didn't have his collar on right. But I asked him one day, "Dr. Grey, how in the world have you been able to get along with a bunch of hardnosed Baptist deacons as long as you have?" "Well," he said, "You know, that reminds me of the time that the old man had lived to be 100 years old, and a reporter who went out to interview him said, 'Well, now, this is a wonderful thing that you have lived a century. What do you consider to be the most wonderful thing that has happened to you? What are you most proud of?' 'Well,' he said, 'The fact that I have lived 100 years, and I don't have any enemies.' 'Oh,' he said, 'that is marvelous. How did that happen?' 'Well,' he said, 'I outlived all of them.'" Then I asked one day, "Dr. Grey, do you think that the First Baptist Church will be able to continue after a while when the years have gone by and you are here no longer?" He replied, "That reminds me of the time that the insurance agent was talking to a man, an old farmer, about taking out more life insurance. Finally, exasperated, he said, 'Old man, do you think you know how your wife is going to be able to carry on after you're gone?' Quickly the man retorted, 'I don't care how she carries on after I am gone, as long as she carries on all right while I am alive.'" So, this is the way Dr. Grey has been, and that's the way I am sure that this church will continue to be through the years that lie ahead.

J. D. Grey has been a practical ecumenist. He has been realistic. He was in 1957 the President of the Federation of Churches in Greater New Orleans. He has served on numerous committees and commissions. He has been one of the wisest counsellors we have

had in every respect, and, as has been said before, I would rather
have him on our side than a good part of the rest of the community
because his wisdom, his counsel, his advice have always been marvelous. The Board of the Greater New Orleans Federation of
Churches has asked me on their behalf and on behalf of the other
135 member congregations of the Greater New Orleans Federation of Churches on this occasion of this 30th Anniversary to
make a presentation to Dr. Grey which reads: "Certificate of
Recognition presented to Dr. J. D. Grey for outstanding and meritorious service in the Cause of Christ's universal kingdom as
expressed through the Greater New Orleans Federation of
Churches."

In the parade of speakers Monsignor Charles J. Plauche,
Chancellor of the Archdiocese of New Orleans, added his
testimony at the anniversary celebration:

Dr. and Mrs. Grey and dear friends, it is with pride and a great
sense of privilege that I stand before you to say a word of appreciation to Dr. Grey for all his years of service in New Orleans;
and I say these words on behalf of three archbishops, one whom I
served for many years, Archbishop Rummel, the one who has left
us for the frozen north, and our present Archbishop Philip M.
Hannan. Archbishops come and go, but Baptists ministers at First
Baptist keep rolling along.

The Bishops of New Orleans and the clergy, the religious and
the Catholic people have over your 30 years here, Dr. Grey, come
to value you very much for your civic endeavors in so many fields;
for your great social consciousness in caring after the spirit of
Jesus for the poor, the halt, the lame, and the blind; for your
prodigious drive as an executive and administrator; and for your
sincere, dedicated religious zeal. We trust that the Lord in His
mercy will have many, many more years of great service in store
for you. We are sure that the First Baptist Church in New Orleans will continue to be a citadel of the ecumenical spirit.

As Dr. Feibelman and others have indicated, we live in a magnificent age when the spirit of friendship and understanding
among those who believe in Christ and among those who believe
in God is taking root as it has not for perhaps 2,000 years or

more. Each denomination is committed in a different way to this spirit and there are varying approaches and degrees, but certainly one would be blind not to see that in the day that is here with us there is much more of the understanding that is needed than we have ever known, than perhaps the world has ever known. And for this as well as your qualities as a pastor of your own denomination and head of the Southern District [Grey didn't quite get Southern Baptist Convention structures across to Monsignor Plauche] at one time, I would like to commend you most humbly and most sincerely, Dr. Grey. Now we learned this morning in the newspaper, but haven't seen the document yet, that our church is just about ready to sing the last requiem for the language that gave us the word *requiem*, the old venerable Latin language, and after a few months we will start saying all of the mass in the vernacular tongues throughout the world, but I would like to close all the same with just a little phrase from the Latin that Dr. Grey will translate for you at his leisure, in case you didn't do too well in Latin in high school, and would like simply to say with all of the sincerity in the world from the bottom of my heart, "Dr. J. D. Grey, God bless you 'Ad Multos Annos'."

Parenthetically, in 1967, J. D.'s Baptist basso was the first Baptist preacher's voice heard in historic St. Louis Cathedral in 150 years. Dr. Penrose St. Amant in his *Short History of Louisiana Baptists* reveals that 1817 was the last time a Baptist had spoken there, and that was the time William B. Johnson, then president of the Triennial Convention and later to be the first president of the Southern Baptist Convention, preached in behalf of the female orphan's society to hundreds in St. Louis Cathedral. The curtain closed and did not open again until the fresh ecumenical winds of change began to blow. Then it was that J. D. was asked to participate in a wedding in July of 1967. He had hoped to write an article about this breakthrough into brotherhood, but his recent dashes to the hospital forbade his doing so. He recalls, however: "I did participate. Later I was an honored guest at the funeral of the late Bishop Joseph Francis Rummel, invited by the Chancellery of the Archdiocese to sit in a special section. I was close enough to his coffin to touch it. He and I were very close friends."

Practical ecumenist Grey, the point-maker, has related for a number of years the following old story, with fresh emphasis: "Dr. Wilfred Grenfell, the famed medical missionary to Labrador, once called upon a woman who suffered from tuberculosis of the ankle, and the doctor found it necessary to amputate her leg. A short time later the great doctor made a brief lecture tour of the United States, and, while speaking in a Congregational church, asked if anyone knew of a person who might donate an artificial leg to the needy Labrador woman. At the close of the meeting a Methodist woman told the doctor that her husband, a Presbyterian, had died and left a wooden leg in good condition. Dr. Grenfell accepted the gift of the leg and later fitted it to the native of Labrador. He said, "When I, an Episcopalian, took that Presbyterian leg, given to me by a Methodist in a Congregational church, back to Labrador, it fitted my Roman Catholic friend, and she could walk." [1]

Grey adds, "That makes us united brethren."

Somewhere Baptists established a reputation for demonstrating their independence by not cooperating. J. D. is convinced there is a better way. In an evangelistic conference in Little Rock, Arkansas, he declared: "I am exercising my Baptist independence when I choose to cooperate with my brethren in a great program of advance along all lines that our Baptist denomination is moving.

"Perhaps that's not an entirely new idea, though it may be expressed somewhat differently from what we have been accustomed to hearing. It does approach our Baptist independence from a different angle than usually heard in Baptist circles. It should be said that to exercise one's independence in choosing to cooperate is at least as Baptistic as to exercise one's Baptist independence in refusing to cooperate. We would consider the choice to cooperate more genuinely and scripturally Baptistic than to choose not to cooperate.

"As a matter of practical fact, our independence is greatly limited. Political independence would mean that one refuses to cooperate with his fellow citizen in trying to achieve political justice; social independence is greatly limited. Political independence would mean that one refuses to cooperate with his fellow citizen in trying to achieve political justice; social independence would mean that one refuses to assume any social responsibilities; economic independence would mean that one declines to share economic responsibilities. Such reasoning runs through all of life's activities and relationships. But to achieve such independence one would become a hermit, cut off entirely from the rest of the world. Every person is involved in the political structure of his country, in the social life of the community and the nation, in the economic affairs of the nation. To realize the greatest personal benefit from all these relationships, one must cooperate with his fellow citizens.

"By the same logic a person cannot realize and experience the highest values of his Christian experience in complete isolation from other Christian people. It is only by banding together and cooperating that we may be able to realize the full benefits and blessings of our Christianity, and it is only in cooperation that we are able to carry out the commissions of Christ."

"Mr. Baptist," however, seldom lets an opportunity slip by when he can gig the "separated" brethren. He and others crossed comic swords recently at an ecumenical luncheon in

New Orleans. The question arose as to which church Christ would belong if he were on earth. A Presbyterian brother asserted, "I think He would join our church because of our deep bedrock convictions"; "I think," chimed in the Methodist brother, "He would join the Methodist church because of our heartfelt religion"; the Catholic father-brother added, "I think He would have to join the Catholic church because of our beautiful ritualism." The three turned and eyed the Grey Dove of Peace who drawled, "Well, to be honest, I don't think He would want to make a change."

And in his characteristic fashion, Shakespeare has an appropriate word for the occasion:

> The wolves have prey'd; and look, the gentle day,
> Before the wheels of Phoebus, round about
> Dapples the drowsy East with spots of Grey.

William Shakespeare

# EYEBALL TO EYEBALL

## WITH CITY HALL

## AND BEYOND

*In a government of the people, by the people, and for the people, politics is the business of everybody.*[1]

Roger S. Shinn

*We can ease our irresponsibility in great causes around us by disparaging the overzealous activity of others.*[2]

Wayne E. Oates

*Christian commitment to the lordship of Jesus Christ means involvement in, not withdrawal from, all the great issues of life. Citizenship is certainly one of those major issues demanding this involvement in today's world. To fail to take seriously the obligations of citizenship would be to ignore a whole world of grave responsibility with which Christians have been entrusted by the Lord of all life. While citizenship is every citizen's job, there is a special sense in which it is the Christian citizen's job.*[3]

Foy Valentine

*The citizen who bears the name of Christian, but whose political involvement is no different from that of the non-Christian, simply must have a counterfeit Christianity.*[4]

Daniel R. Grant

*The real problem may be not so much that politicians aren't Christian enough but that Christians aren't political enough. In order to have Christian statesmanship, it is essential for those citizens interested in Christian statesmanship to learn how to be more politically effective. The so-called "unbridgeable gulf" between the spirit of Christ and the spirit of politics will disappear in a democracy if even an active minority of Christian citizens will become masters of the fine arts of politics.*[5]

Daniel R. Grant

# VIGNETTE 7

*If you can talk with crowds and keep your virtue,*
*Or walk with Kings—nor lose the common touch.*

## SHADES OF GREY

Saint J. D. has operated under the theory that if politics are dirty, then add the detergent of Christian ethics. He has a long laundry list.

The saint is of the persuasion that citizens, and especially Christian citizens, have the responsibility of keeping the light of public opinion focused on politics generally and politicians specifically; that the best way to make a politician see the light is to make him feel the heat. The news media are not exempt; they must be encouraged to keep the searchlight on all political activities. He believes, furthermore, some politicians act under the mistaken notion that they have been anointed rather than elected. The doctrine of the divine right of rulers dissipated too quickly to suit their purposes. All too frequently, while a statesman believes he belongs to the people in his responsibility to them, a politician thinks the people belong to him for all he can take. "These are my people" is to J. D. a thin veil to hide exploitation and cynical disregard for public service. Some act as if they are indispensable. Adam, they say, was indispensable; but, of course, observes the Saint, that was before our time. Besides, Adam may have been the first politican to take a bite out of the public apple. Paradise has been in the speeches but out of reach of these public men ever since.

Grey has bemoaned the fact that all too often ninety percent of the politicians have made the other ten percent look bad. He is not naive to the point that he does not accept the fact that politicians have clay feet, just as saints do. Consequently, he can echo the retort of the councilman who, in an anonymous call from one of his constituents, was scolded with great emotion, "I want you to know that if you were St. Peter I wouldn't vote for you in the next election." The councilman kept his cool and calmly shut her out with, "Lady, if I were St. Peter, you wouldn't even be in my precinct."

Let's keep it straight for the Saint: We the people elect the presidents, governors, mayors, dog-catchers, but not the critics. They appoint themselves. Politicians, to be sure, are guilty of gross sins upon the people, but disaster follows upon the heels of the critic who is satisfied to sit in some penthouse of safety and clip his political coupons. There can be no absentee ownership in a democracy, in Grey's thinking. Let the people who own rich soil of government care enough to plow and seed and weed if they want an honest harvest.

To seek the kingdom of righteousness, according to Grey, is not to begin by burning offerings to "quo status," that ancient god. "If Jesus had preferred the status quo to God's will, there would have been no Calvary. If Luther had valued unity over truth, there might not have been a Reformation. If the patriots of 1776 had treasured peace more than principle, there would have been no United States of America." [6]

Would not a saint deplore the excuses given for not being a full citizen? To be preoccupied is not a valid excuse for non-involvement. Those loyal yet look-alike citizens with flag in hand would profess that they are not against democracy and the American way of life. H. G. Wells caught the attitude in the words of one of his novels: "I don't care. The world may be going to pieces. The Stone Age may be returning. This, as you say, may be the sunset of civilization. I'm sorry, but I can't help it this morning. I have other engagements. All the same—laws of the Medes and Persians— I'm going to play croquet with my aunt at half-past twelve today."

Excuses, in Grey's opinion, serve only to weaken the American dream of democratic involvement—a dream rather than a reality if we do not work at it. God has not guaranteed that the American experiment will succeed without human "blood, sweat, and tears." The rapid advance of the computer age has not transformed democracy into the end result of a few men's programming. It is people, not robots, who make the whole thing work.

Again, to shift the blame in matters political is self-deception, thinks Grey. In exasperation, one college president has said, "After thirty years as a college president, I have not been able to ascertain whether a B. A. stands for Bachelor of Arts or Builder of Alibis."

J. D. (Justifying Defender) says that not all Christians are lifeless to their civic duties, but many of them are alive and hiding in the church. He contends one funeral is long overdue—that of the so-called innocent bystander. Too many people are guilty of subversive inactivity, which to our silver-toned saint is a criminal act. Detachment from the world is hardly a Christian virtue—either for an individual or for a church. There is no valid nor acceptable reason for not being involved as a citizen. To criticize without involvement is to default. To vote and to pay taxes are the means to an end, not an end in themselves. To retreat or to treat politics as a philosophical leprosy is to abandon the power structures to nonexistent spiritual dimensions. Non-involvement cancels the privilege of infallible pontification.

The Grey one further amplifies that politics involve confrontation with an imperfect world where the choice is never between black and white but between varying shades of gray. Criticism is an escape mechanism to avoid acceptance of responsibility, a form of generalized irresponsibility. Without recognition of moral and civic measurements we are often deceived by the false freedom of "living our own lives." Citizenship is indeed the bloodstream of community life. Pretense, smug self-righteousness, and social community blindness contribute to lawlessness. It has been said that "civilization is like a little clearing on the edge of the jungle—and at night, if you are quiet, you can hear the howling of the beasts; and the jungle is always waiting, ready to take over the minute man relaxes his vigilance." To illustrate, Germany in 1930 was a center of learning, but in the span of a few years it became the arena of atrocities and indecencies which shocked the world.

Let no man wait for the church to speak all his mind, for "the churches," says Roger Shinn, "should be more cautious than individuals or groups of Christians in taking political stands. Christians, especially churches, should be more ready to make pronouncements on issues than on candidates —always recognizing that times come when issues and men are inseparable. Christian judgments should never stem solely from the clergy but should involve lay specialists with skill in public affairs.

"The church is in this world as an agent of God's redemption, and the world infiltrates the church. The world is where God located the church, where God expects it to fulfill its mission, where men must be obedient as they fulfill their ministries.

"But the great and abiding work remains. It is for the church to produce men—Christian men—honest men—wise men—dedicated men, and to thrust them forth to serve their

Lord in the service of the state. If this fails, church and nation both suffer." [7]

The Grey question—detachment or engagement, escape or involvement, the sidelines or the stands—which is it to be?

As a citizen one may be disenchanted with politics in general, but the world cannot afford the luxury of one spiritual dropout. If this course of inaction is chosen, does one have the right to criticize the hippies? They do not protest at all but simply smile, wave daffodils, and act like lilies of field— who seek not to change society but simply have nothing to do with it.

On the occasion of the twenty-fifth anniversary of J. D. as pastor of First Baptist Church, Brooks Hays, another former president of the Southern Baptist Convention and, at the time, special assistant to President John F. Kennedy, saluted our man in the Crescent City for his direct action involvement in the total life: "He demonstrates faith in our political system. He believes in separation of church and state, but he believes the bridges of understanding must be built across the chasm that sometimes divides the religious and political areas of life. He believes that there must be commerce in ideas; that the political community must have the wholesome influence of religious ideas.

"His eloquent voice is raised for civic righteousness, but always in love, never in hatred. He believes in the oneness of the human family."

R. A. Tawney, the British historian, calls to mind the English nobleman of a hundred years ago who became greatly irritated by the preaching to which he listened. "Things have come to a pretty pass," he said, "when religion is allowed to interfere with a man's private life." We can hear his modern family cry still, "Things have come to a pretty pass if religion is going to move out into the fields of economics, politics, and international affairs." If these areas need redemption, then the minister of the God of redemption must be there.

How? J. D. (Judicious Deputy) has constantly vocalized the how of the minister's responsibility before school, church, civic, and service organizations. "It is inspiring to note that the truly great people in life who have achieved eminence and have made lasting contributions to the glory of God and the betterment of mankind have been those who were motivated by a great formula of action. Believing and achieving always go together."

"Let us begin with a simple ballot," he continues. "When you become of voting age, it is yours to use to select those you would have to govern you. Since our government 'derives its just powers from the consent of the governed,' this ballot will be the means by which you select those who are to rule over you. It is the foe of tyranny and demagoguery in every form. It is the bulwark of our American civilization and the guarantee of our democratic processes. Use this power which the ballot symbolizes and use it well. Become an intelligent citizen who participates in all the affairs of his government from the election of a justice of the peace to the President of the United States. As long as free men use this ballot well our future as a nation is secure."

His mythical Uncle Zeke from Alabama nailed it down when asked if he believed in using voting machines. "Nope," he answered, "I think the people ought to vote."

Our Judicious Deputy has observed that machine politics result when people leave the decisions to the computers. When there is such widespread reluctance to vote, there is also little eagerness to meet the other demands of politics. Defaulting at the polls lets politics fall into the hands of those who, as often as not, are primarily concerned with advancing their own interests.

The right to vote and influence public affairs is a right hard won by our forefathers, who committed their lives, their fortunes, and their sacred honor to win political independence and representative government. Percy Hayward stated it recently in "Meditation Beside a Ballot Box": "It took a thousand years to shape this box. Only by centuries of struggle was that lock fastened upon it to preserve my ballot in honor. One generation of men after another beat themselves against the door to this room, and died upon the threshold before it opened to let me in to choose my government. Dreamers and poets of liberty, martyrs and prophets of truth, soldiers and seamen, statesmen and philosophers, all who have labored and suffered in the costly human march toward freedom—these are my unseen companions beside the ballot box today." [8]

Yet there is more room among the shades of Grey, for Christians can become machines if they are content only to pull a lever. The political involvement of the preacher is not fulfilled in Sabbath-morning prayers, or verbal fireworks of condemnation upon occasions, or equating Christianity and democracy, or pretending that political life exists only on the national scene so that the local situation never comes to life graphically.

Politics require attention to issues as well as to men, and it falls upon the pulpit man to be the issue man also. He must inform his congregation of the issues and his convictions about the issues, and he must encourage them to be informed, even risking that their further information may supersede his own. He ought to be at least that secure. Harold Macmillan says, "I have never found in a long experience in politics that criticism was ever inhibited by ignorance."

If our sole political exercise is pulling a lever or making our mark, then let Pavlov's dog with his programmed salivation do the job for us. Ring the right bell, turn on the right light, emit the right odor, and "Bing!"—another vote for the biscuit man.

### In the Arena

Theodore Roosevelt once said: "It is not the critic who counts, or how the strong man stumbled and fell, or where the doer of deeds could have done them better. The credit belongs to the man who is actually in the arena, whose face is marred by dust and sweat and blood, who strives valiantly, who errs and comes short again and again, who knows the great enthusiasms, the great devotion, and spends himself in a worthy cause; and if he fails, at least fails while daring greatly, so that he'll never be with those cold and timid souls who know neither victory nor defeat!"

The relationship between J. D and the arena is more than semantic. Arena is the Spanish word for sand, which covered the surfaces of the ancient coliseums, where men fought men and beasts for the entertainment of thousands, and where thousands of Christians dramatically gave witness to their faith. J. D. knows what it means to step down into the sand—the arena—and illustrate his concept of Christianity. "A man," he said, "will share his religion with everyone he meets. He will take it into his home, his business, and his politics."

Moses stood before Pharaoh, Nathan before David, Elijah before Ahab, Christ before Pilate. If these could not escape the encounter, how can the followers of Jesus expect to? Is the servant greater than the Master?

Hear the word from the sand: "A few months after I arrived in New Orleans, I started preaching against gambling and speaking against corruption in City Hall, criticising the mayor, Bob Maestri. My position was generally known, for I had spoken out against gambling and corruption. One day a very prominent and wealthy New Orleans man who was Catholic, with relatives in our church, called me and said, 'Reverend Grey, I'd like to get acquainted with you. I wonder if you would do me the honor of going to lunch with me.' I said, 'Well, Mr. So and So, I would be indeed delighted to go with you. Thank you, sir.'

"We met downtown at the place we had agreed upon and had a very nice lunch. He was very gracious and complimentary of the way I was beginning my ministry. He told me a little about his relationship to the church through his relative. Then he said, 'But, Reverend Grey, New Orleans is different from Texas. There are a lot of things accepted here that I am sure you didn't have in Texas—like a little innocent gambling, like people rolling dice for the check, double or nothing, at the restaurants, or the hotel cigar counters.' He said, 'I'd like to suggest if you want to do well here, and make a success of this church, and become a religious leader, that you just sort of soft-pedal these things and forget about them.' He said, 'We've got a wonderful mayor who is doing great things for New Orleans. He asked me about you and would like to meet you.' You know, the man went on to say, 'The mayor goes out in his limousine with his chauffeur every day to inspect the various WPA projects such as street and building improvements that we have in New Orleans, and he wanted to come by some morning to take you on a tour and get acquainted.'

"Well, I was a bit cagey; I didn't know just how to answer. I knew I wasn't interested in going with this politician to see these things and perhaps get under obligation to him. I said, 'Well, maybe it could be arranged.' So that broke up the conversation—but needless to say, I paid no attention to his warning and his advice. He wasn't threatening; he was just trying to give me some Dutch-uncle advice which I didn't accept in any sense.

"As a corollary to this incident was a situation that developed soon after: the old church at St. Charles and Delachaise had acquired a house and lot next door—one with a back yard. When we spoke of wanting to develop it into a playground and volleyball and basketball court for our young people, one of our men said that the city would be glad to pave it under a WPA project. I was amazed that one or two of the men who advocated it failed to realize that we would be accepting tax monies as a church. When I said very strongly that I would resist it, these brethren who hadn't thought about the implications soon capitulated, and we did our own paving. Through the years I have taken my stand on matters involving tax funds for sectarian purposes because we had resisted efforts to get hooked, as it were, on that first proposition. And that's one thing I have said to our Baptist and Protestant groups here in the city over the years—that we must not compromise in any manner, or get under obligation to any officials or any governmental agency by accepting tax monies."

Thus Judicious Defender learned early in his ministry that if a person compromises with politicians by accepting government favors for public silence he has painted himself into the corner of their contempt. The compromiser is as wise as the stowaway on a kamikaze plane; he is a born loser.

One of his earliest excursions in "getting to know them" occurred in connection with inauguration of Earl K. Long as governor of the State of Louisiana. The governor took as his inaugural text: "Righteousness Exalteth a Nation." Grey in turn preached a sermon the following Sunday morning from the same scripture. He sent the governor a telegram informing him of his intention and inviting him to attend. The invitation was respectfully declined, but J. D. still got the message in the Monday morning edition of the *Times Picayune,* which gave front page coverage to the message and his advice to the new governor.

The colorful Uncle Earl remained an admirer of J. D.'s for a long time. Witness his homiletical preference in a remark to a mutual friend: "Everybody's bragging about this Billy Graham. Hell! He can't preach nothing like J. D. Grey. I had rather hear him preach than any man I've ever heard."

Mayors have known and heard him. One of the significant friend-critic relationships J. D. formed was with the late Chep Morrison, a suave New Orleans Roman Catholic, who was leader of the city for three terms. On occasion J. D. raked his friend over the coals in matters political and controversial. His influence was effective on many issues. By the same token, the mayor could respond to J. D. as a friend when he offered, without prejudice, the keys to the city to a young Billy Graham in his first crusade in the City That Care Forgot.

J. D. saw in Morrison gubernatorial timber and in a note professed, "I believe you would make us the best governor we could find now." The next morning a member of the mayor's staff called and related that Morrison was deeply touched by the letter of encouragement and requested permission to use the letter. A rueful J. D. remembers, "Well, many times I take off without getting my mule hitched up. I didn't say how to use it. I said, 'Why, of course, you can use it.' I thought he meant he would quote me in a news release.

"By George, the full text of the letter came out in every

paper in Louisiana, half page and full page ads. The first call I got was from a woman who said: 'I want you to tell me what your name is.' I said, 'Well, my name is J. D. Grey.' She said, 'It isn't. It's Martin Luther King.' Wham! Hung up. God is my witness, that was the first instant I ever imagined anybody would drag the race question into that letter I wrote Chep."

In addition to numerous calls, he received a shopping bag full of letters of protest over the use of the letter. "Basically," J. D. recalls, "I did not believe that Chep Morrison was the greatest guy who ever came down the pike. I knew there were certain things that were unexplained about him. But I felt that it was unfair to crucify him in North Louisiana because he was a Catholic from New Orleans."

In defense of Grey, Rabbi Leo A. Bergman stated in the afternoon edition of the *New Orleans Item*:

It is time for people of all religions to join together for a better world, and he defended the right of a minister to speak out on politics as a means of improving the state.

Need pastors be silent?

Politics cannot be divorced from life; politics is life. Whether the politics are local, state, or federal, politics are synonymous with life. Religion is part of life. It is part of life or nothing at all.

People are shocked when men of religion have the nerve to speak, he said.

Preachers are only expected to console the hurt, perform the wedding ceremonies, administer the services of the church, pity the downtrodden.

We do not want to upset the status quo. But this is a difficult period in our history.

Friendships have not deterred Grey from criticising men in public office, nor has he exhibited a party spirit; in fact, he has been more harsh with his fellow Baptists in political life than with any others.

The word comes again from the sand. In speaking to public groups, civic clubs, Chamber of Commerce meetings, and business conventions, J. D. has warned of the easy tolerance of public corruption.

Kiwanians in Greenwood, Mississippi, heard him: "Cheap, tinhorn politicians are subject to easy bribery and corruption. . . . If you think bribery ends with gambling, whiskey, and vice, you are dead wrong. The same officials who can be bribed to permit these violations can be bribed to permit robbery, murder, and other crimes."

In 1942, those attending a flag dedication service in the First Baptist Church heard him read an open letter to Mayor Robert S. Maestri's reiteration that gambling must stop in the city. The *Times Picayune* picked it up: "Mr. Maestri," Dr. Grey wrote, "those orders have not been carried out. You either have among your subordinates a group who are disloyal to you and defiant to your orders, or you have a group who ignores your authority. Mr. Mayor, the integrity of your office is at stake. If you have a police department, a district attorney that positively ignores or definitely refuses to do what you tell them, then you should get a set of officers who will do as you say."

For the last quarter of a century, since the closing days of World War II, J. D. has gone everywhere on speaking engagements, jabbing men awake to their responsibilities in keeping the flame of liberty burning. Eternal vigilance is the price of freedom—complete freedom is the ideal of our American way of life. It includes not only political and economic freedom, but also religious freedom. . . . America must build her strongest line of defense in the heart and the spirit of her people.

"Liberty—let's keep it. Let that liberty encompass all the freedoms which we enjoy in our great and glorious America:

freedom of religion, freedom of speech, freedom of the press, and freedom of the ballot box. Many freedoms have been lost because people have not exercised them. Our American freedoms must be maintained, thus keeping our nation as one of the few remaining islands of freedom in the great sea of totalitarianism where all liberty is lost."

**THE**

**SECOND LOUISIANA**

**PURCHASE**

*Assume direct personal responsibility for the moral world which surrounds you, for you can never delegate responsibility . . .*

Tolstoy

*When sense of obligation to God and to community disappear, then irresponsibility will soon raise its serpent head. It is but a short step from indifference to assault.*[1]

Albert McClellan

# VIGNETTE 8

*If you can make one heap of all your winnings,*
*And risk it on one turn of pitch-and-toss.*

SHADES OF GREY

The saint has a bee in his halo when it comes to crime and gambling, or as he says, "I've got ants in my pants as big as cockroaches." Preacher words, no doubt, except that in Steel Grey's case, he puts iron into his words by his actions.

If he needs to justify his energetic involvement, he has only to describe the scene he sees through his spiritual microscope. He is like a man watching bacteria multiply on a slide, and he does not like what he sees, for he sees crime and gambling as a blight on and a sin against society. They are destructive of home, for they humiliate self-respect, impoverish means, blast happiness, and destroy love. They are destructive of brotherhood, for they deny its essential spirit; the gain of the criminal is his brother's loss. They are destructive of clean athletics. Wherever the gambler and his Black Hand boys go in, clean sport goes out. They are destructive of business, because they can render no services, produce no goods, create no wealth. They are like dogs trying to feed on their own tails. They are destructive of government and the state, for they provide the main sources of bribery, graft, and the debauchery of public service.

Gambling hurts—that is the salient fact in the mind of J. D. It hurts many people and it is indiscriminate in its results. The children it spawns are named "lack of integrity," "loss of affection," "debt," and "delinquency."

Grey has focused upon this plague in the laboratory of his pulpit and life as he reasons that man was created in community. Crime and gambling disrupt community. Man becomes true man in the intricate interactions of society, and in these human personality is achieved and nourished. When the orderly social processes and dependable relationships are weakened, says J. D., every man suffers. From the Old Testament and the New Testament come the approaches of law and love as supports to a community. The bacteria which terrify the social order are the enemies of both law and love.

Gambling is morally wrong, the iron Grey man contends, because it hurts society, it hurts its individual victims, and it hurts the economy because it produces nothing and adds nothing to the welfare of the people. Eloquent arguments may be advanced to justify the presence of the gambling virus, but no society that bases its financial structure on hurting its people deserves to survive.

Grey has heard the big lie, "If you can't lick evil, then legalize it," but he has never been too fond of letting yesterday's lies become tomorrow's truths. He knows that when there is no watchman at the gates, the thieves will slink in and steal out—all they can. One does not wonder then why he plays an active role as a member of the all-important Governor's Commission on Law Enforcement and Administration of Criminal Justice.

He has formed a long Grey line at the gates of his city, his state, and his nation, organizing groups of concerned citizens who will throw out the garbage before it drives out the people by its rotten odor. The first meeting of those who would eventually found the Louisiana Moral and Civic

Foundation took place in the pastor's study in the First Baptist Church of New Orleans. As one of the attending and vitally interested doctors at its birth, he has watched his LMCF baby grow up. For years he has been on the board of the Metropolitan Crime Commission of the city of New Orleans. When asked why he would allow himself to be saddled with the presidency, now for his second term, he answered, "Because for thirty years in this town I have gotten tired of seeing competent laymen who would shirk their responsibilities. The job had to be done; somebody has to take a stand. Who am I that I should be spared because I am a man of the cloth? I have a constant battle with myself as I think about these two hats that I must wear. If I go to a news conference now, or if I am interviewed or called on the phone, I wonder which hat I am wearing, that of the pastor of the First Baptist Church or that of the president of the Crime Commission. Generally the answer is both of them. Yet they are not the same hat, because I don't want the image of the Crime Commission established as a preacher do-good organization."

The fraternity of the cloth often justifies its non-involvement in critical social issues by convincing itself that the people least impressed are those who should be most impressed—the underworld. The question on this part of the test then is True or False: Does the criminal element take notice of citizens' concern and action against crime and gambling? Answer: True!

Called to the witness stand was the underworld character in New Orleans who lashed out at those who tried to straighten a crooked society. He concluded by asking, "Who do they think they are? They're just a bunch of damn citizens!" To his disgust he inadvertently gave a title to a motion picture produced by Universal-International Pictures.

As he researched the subject of crime and gambling in Louisiana, Herman Webber, the producer, kept seeing J. D.'s name pop up as one who opposed vice. He contacted J. D. and insisted that he play a minor role in the movie. "My part," said J. D., "concerned Colonel Francis Grevemberg, after he had been appointed by Governor Kennon to head the State Police, coming to my office for my advice. The film portrayed that conversation in which I advised him to have courage and take the job." He was further involved when he furnished clippings and data to the story writers and allowed shots of First Baptist Church to appear in the movie. At first J. D. had some reservations about the picture's title, "Damn Citizen," feeling that it might alienate some folks. It was then he learned from Mr. Webber of the remark made by the unwitting crook which entitled the picture. Somehow Grey's name was left off the Oscar award nominations for the year, but his reward continues to be a deep personal satisfaction that he can be counted among those "damn" citizens.

The underworld may call him a dirty rat (this is one of the nicer euphemisms) but they know he's not a mouse Grey. They receive him like mice who all jump on chairs when a scabrous female walks into a room.

He has been a target for the not-so-subtle barbs of the gambling supporters as he moves about the city. His occasional appearances on television for the Crime Commission have provoked the question, "Well, how's the television star?" which generally receives the answer, "Oh, you watch the late horror shows, huh?"

Grey tones were heard early on the subject of gambling. One of his first sermons in New Orleans was "Keeping New Orleans Constantly Clean," and he was not simply trying to echo the beautification association's slogan, "Every litter bit hurts." He was after a more personalized garbage. The Chamber of Commerce, upon announcing their proposed campaign to clean up New Orleans, said, "Let's get the trash, the litter up off the street." And they wrote all the pastors a letter and asked them to give a deliverance on it. "So I grabbed that. I had been there a month, and I was quite shocked at seeing little kids held up by their parents to pull the levers of slot machines; at seeing business men roll the dice with the cashier as to whether they would pay double or nothing on their check at most respectable hotels, cigar-counters, and restaurants.

"I announced that I was going to preach next Sunday night on 'Keeping New Orleans Constantly Clean and Completely Clean.' I wrote a letter to the President of the Chamber of Commerce, to the Executive Secretary, to the Mayor, and to a dozen people and invited them to hear my sermon. I was cooperating with the clean-up campaign, and I wanted them to hear my sermon on it. A number of the prominent businessmen of New Orleans were there, and they have been friends of mine through the years. I ripped into the issue. I told them, 'Why, sure, we want to get this garbage cleaned up. Let's not drop litter on the streets. Let's go a step further.' You see, I hit this town being articulate on issues that I think a preacher ought to stand for in the community.

"I haven't had to stand alone. I have drafted my men into the Grey line. The men of the church have supported me in these scraps I have been in with the underworld, with crime, and with public officials—how my men stood up! I never shall forget the threatening letters I got on my first excursion in this field—one especially very, very ominous letter, very threatening. One Sunday morning I said to Herman Hitt, Watson Merritt, and a couple of others, 'I've got something I must talk to somebody about this afternoon.' We went to Mr. Hitt's house.

"Three men and I sat in the car while I told them about this letter and others like it. Then I said, 'I am going to have to make up my mind, and I want you to help me do it. Shall I be a nice little Lord Fauntleroy and preach little palliatives here and pleasing sermons there, be a popular guy whom everybody loves and nobody criticizes? Or shall I take a gutty stand on these issues that come up, even with threats?' To a man, these gentlemen said, 'You do what you think you ought to do. We are proud of you, and the stands you have taken. We'll back you to the point of physical defense or provide protection for you if it is necessary.' I said, 'Do you feel that others in the church beside you share that view?' They said, 'Everybody we know; we know them well enough to guarantee to you that this is the way they feel about it.' And since that time there have never been any really dangerous physical threats made against me."

The note sounded early has continued to be a part of the concert of his preaching as he has spoken out against vice and gambling. The excerpts from these sermons read like a staccato rendition of the "Flight of the Gamble Bee" or the "Anvil Chorus."

Addressing the Louisiana Baptist Convention, J. D. declared himself a grateful beneficiary of the First Louisiana Purchase and unalterably opposed to the Second. The first brought Louisiana into the United States. The second threatens to sell Louisiana to the gambling interests in and out of the state. The first brought his city into his nation, but the second is an epidemic which could strangle both city and nation. He thankfully salutes the first, but the second will receive his energetic wrath until the last dice lie cold upon unused felt.

Does it seem paradoxical, then, that a friend could say about Iron Grey: "J. D. definitely isn't a tea-sipper, and if I were choosing out of all the Southern Baptist Convention someone to walk down a dark alley with me—someone that I think would fight to the end with me and give and ask no quarter—I think I would choose J. D."

*Grey Shadows*

> This I learned from the shadow of a tree
> That to and fro did sway upon a wall—
> My shadow, my influence, may fall
> Where I may never be.
>
> Anonymous

**LOOSE FOOTBALL**

*Paul Dietzel tells that after becoming coach of Army, when Army lost to Navy, he was so downcast that he wanted to call his wife to get a few words of love and affection to massage his ego. Not having any change, he turned to an Army cadet and said, "Lend me a dime to call a friend." The cadet gave him twenty cents and said, "Call all of your friends."*

Duke K. McCall

*He always generates a lot of excitement around him. He does not so much go where the action is as he seems to create the action—or to put it another way, action goes where he goes.*

Frank Norfleet

# VIGNETTE 9

*If you can fill the unforgiving minute*
*with sixty seconds' worth of distance run.*

## SHADES OF GREY

The New Orleans *Times-Picayune* of December 28, 1956, previewing the anticipated clash between Baylor and Tennessee in the Sugar Bowl, recalled an earlier "conflict of spiritual interest" in which J. D. (Joking dazzling) was Saturday's hero. It was 1951. "The Bear" Bryant was bringing his Kentucky Wildcats into the Sugar Bowl to meet Mr. Nice's (Bud Wilkinson's) Oklahoma Sooners.

Before the game, J. D. led in prayer—the first pregame prayer in the history of the Sugar Bowl. Kentucky won. A few days after the game Herschel Hobbs, a close personal friend who favored the Sooners, wrote: "I'm going to protest to the Sugar Bowl Committee because you prayed, and you're from Kentucky. They ought to have had somebody from Oklahoma pray." The answer was short and to the point: "I don't think we ought to worry the Lord about a little thing like that. With Babe Parilli on our team we didn't need to worry the Lord."

Sooner supporters should have been forewarned when J. D. remarked at a 1949 showing of the film of the Sugar Bowl whang-doodle between North Carolina and Oklahoma, "I was yelling for North Carolina but praying for Oklahoma." Oklahoma won that one.

J. D. (Jumping Darting) could well appreciate the not-so-hidden despair of Baylor Ex-Students Director, George

*143*

Stokes, who, when asked if he believed in praying for Baylor to win, confessed, "I usually pray: 'Lord, if it is your will let Baylor win. If not—stay out of it!' "

Some might question the effectiveness or worshipfulness of pregame prayers. It would make more sense to reserve the praying for the scrimmage sessions.

These tradition-honored quiet times, however, can be used to focus upon issues more basic than the outcome of an afternoon's gridiron wrestling match. It was during the tense hours of the Korean War that J. D. offered this prayer for peace.

### A Prayer for Peace

Gracious God: We offer thanks to Thee for Thy blessings showered upon our beloved land. We thank Thee for the heritage that is ours as Americans. May we be ever mindful of the glorious tradition which is our blood-bequeathed legacy from the past. Give us, we pray Thee, in this critical hour the true greatness and spiritual strength of our forefathers. Grant wisdom to our leaders and courage to all our people. Be with those who bravely fight for our God-given way of life. Put down the forces of evil. Hasten the day when wars shall be no more and "righteousness shall cover the earth as the waters cover the sea." With forgiveness for our national and individual sins, we beg it in the name of Him who is the Prince of Peace, Amen.

His prayerful association with football continues. The name of J. D. Grey is found on the program of the Second Annual Saints and Sinners Awards Banquet in 1961 when he pronounced the invocation for the New Orleans Football Saints. This is hardly out of character, since he is always praying for the saints—and the sinners.

J. D. is no neophyte to the subtle nuances of the grid wars. In fact, some have analogized his behaviour as being like a loose football. Both always excite a crowd. At any convention you have only to spot a huddle of preachers who seem to be generating their own fuel, and there in the middle is J. D.

What Vince Lombardi is to men charging themselves up for an afternoon game, J. D. is to that first cousin of football—a convention. He is no fumbler when it comes to carrying the ball. He can play any position. He has been coach and quarterback, bringing his keen sense of the fundamentals of the game onto the playing field; giving pep talks when the air hangs heavy with defeat; or leading the cheering section when a score is imminent. He can promote the sale of tickets for the big game or invade the field as trainer and waterboy, to refresh young preachers during time-outs. When their "three yards and cloud of dust" offense has begun to stall with the goal line in view, he can even be seen on the sidelines keeping the exact time on the progress of the current game, or he can go back a quarter-century and more to recite date, time, and place of the gridiron battles in Baptist history. As referee he has blown, and will blow, the whistle on any unsportsmanlike conduct or breach of the game rules. His red flag is quick to appear in instances of personal fouls and unnecessary roughness. With him it isn't whether you win or win—but how you play the game to win. Playing for a tie for him is like receiving the holy kiss from the sister who came down the aisle during the invitation, with matted hair (a stranger to Halo shampoo for milleniums), smeared, uneven lipstick, hemline three inches longer in the back than the front, sagging hose giving indication she had crawled through a barbed wire fence, and whined through her snuff-stained teeth: "I want you to pray for me; my husband's been running around on me!" Echoes of Bear Bryant!

He is always in training, sharpening his game plans with strenuous mental calisthenics. He is expert in the use of isometrics to give tone and shape to spiritual muscles. He can bench press any load—his own and often that of teammates.

His willingness to play offense or defense—backfield or line—is well known. He can throw the bomb or red-dog the opposition into a costly fumble; he can form the protective pocket for the traditional freedoms of Baptist people or rescue his own harried teammates with a game-winning, end-around Statue of Liberty play; he can be lonesome end if principles dictate, or flanker if the signals call for it; he can kick a field goal or block a punt. He can substitute quickly and graciously and can often break open a dull or stalemated game.

After the game is over and the troops wend their weary way back to the steam rooms, he is ready to meet the press with some hot copy. His philosophy is that at no time should a man's public relations have a garlic breath; he should be programmed for a constant public relations response to all occasions—but not with quite the intensity or glory-seeking amateurishness of Moses' apocryphal public relations director. Panic-stricken because of the approaching Egyptians, he said to Moses, "What are you going to do?" Moses replied, "Take it easy. In a few minutes I'm going to stand and raise my hands and part the Red Sea. When the Children of Israel have passed over, I will close the liquid expressway on top of Pharaoh and his ski-less army." The public relations man with great jubilation said, "Moses, if you pull this off, you can be assured I can get you three pages in the Old Testament."

J. D. is like a loose football—floating around conventions, conferences, and seminars looking for where the action is. He is engaging old friends in conversation and available to new friends for fellowship. He is not an untouchable, casting himself above or below other messengers. Of all convention presidents, none has been friendlier or known more people on a first-name basis. He is a circulating Mary Worth, listening to gripes, giving advice and encouragement, taking the temperature of feverish issues and feeling the pulse of the convention in general.

He is like a loose football—tickling the ribs of some sombre brother with the latest anecdote or word-sparring with a close friend. In mock-seriousness J. (Joking) walked up to Pastor Warren Hultgren and inquired, "Warren, what is your revival schedule for next year?" He replied, "I will be glad to check with my secretary when I call her this afternoon." Seriousness gone, J. D. countered, "Good, let me know when you can have me for a meeting."

His mealtimes at conventions are rarely tables for two. There is a train of humanity that expectantly file by, anticipating *the* word on the convention or sharing some delectable morsel of humor. Enjoying an *après shi* dish of coconut ice cream (his favorite) at Howard Johnson's, he was overheard to say, "If my doctor knew I was eating this coconut ice cream, he wouldn't sleep a wink tonight."

J. (Jazzy) is no party pooper, convention or no convention! He loves to stay up as late as the next brother, and will still be the first to hit the floor running the next A.M. for another day of loose footballing.

IF ELECTED—WOULD SERVE

*In my estimation, J. D. Grey is one of the most versatile, knowledgeable, and perceptive men in the ministry. Several years ago, Billy Graham said to me, after Dr. Grey had visited the London Crusade, that Dr. Grey was one of the very few men in the world who could stand on any platform, anywhere, before any crowd, and always do and say the right thing.*

*Here is a man who is first a Christian, secondly a committed Baptist, always the Christian gentleman, and forever the statesman.*

Warren C. Hultgren

*As one of his members at First Church, New Orleans, recently said of him, "Dr. Grey is a great man and a great preacher." It was because they shared this belief that Southern Baptists have twice elected him president of the Southern Baptist Convention.*[1]

Porter Routh

*No man among us has won more distinction among Southern Baptists than J. D. Grey. He has influenced so many groups, has been a friend to all of us.*

W. A. Criswell

*J. D. Grey is a leader—one of those men people respect as a leader for his remarkable talents and skills. He is the kind whom people will inevitably elect to champion the cause. Like John Hill, when J. D. walks into a room, everyone looks at him and knows this is a leader.*

James L. Sullivan

*I remember J. D. well. As a young man he was an orator. We called him Patrick Henry.*

W. C. Jetton

# VIGNETTE 10

*If you can keep your head when all about you*
*Are losing theirs and blaming it on you.*

## SHADES OF GREY

The first time J. D. was nominated for president of the Southern Baptist Convention he was elected. Such a victory was not even predicted by Jeane Dixon. This event, strange as it may seem to us today, took place without the trappings we are accustomed to seeing on television. There were no floor managers, no walkie-talkies, no caucuses, no mobile control centers flush against the auditorium, and no spontaneous hired bands.

Grey's age—he was the youngest nominee ever to be elected president—made him a dark horse. Some good men were in the race, and one of the best, James W. Storer, wrote a follow-up article on the convention which was carried in several Baptist state papers. He noted, "Many people have been beaten by a dark horse. But I was run over by a grey." Storer was elected as president to succeed J. D. in 1953.

Perhaps Storer had in mind the then current story of a brief association with a beatnik and its disastrous conclusion. A salesman driving out West stopped in a moment of misguided compassion to pick up a hitchhiking beatnik. Braking at an intersection, he asked his unwashed passenger if any traffic was coming from the right. "Only a dog, man," was the reply. Pulling out on the highway, the salesman was run over by a large vehicle. When he woke in the hospital, turned, and saw the beatnik encased in a body cast occupying the other bed in the room, he screamed, "What kind of dog were you talking about?" "It was just a dog, man, a Greyhound," was the nonchalant reply.

The question should really be whether or not the Kentucky thoroughbred was running in the Baptist Derby. Ask the man and you get the answer. "One of the delights of being a former president of the Southern Baptist Convention is that you can go into any crowd and shake hands around with everybody there and be friendly without somebody asking, 'What is that fool running for now?' You see, at the Chicago convention in 1950, Herschel Hobbs and I were pictured together in the Chicago papers and tagged as two of the leading contenders for the presidency of the Southern Baptist Convention. I know a lot of people said that we were running, and the same has been said of every man who has ever been nominated. But God is my witness, down in my heart, I kept hoping, 'Well, maybe someday if it's right, I would enjoy being president of the Convention.' But I never talked to a close friend or anybody else and never brought the subject up anywhere to try to influence anybody to guide his thinking that I ought to be nominated or elected.

"In 1951, before we got to San Francisco, one of my wonderful friends from Texas, a seminary classmate, said, 'J. D., you know you're being pushed to be president of the convention?' I said, 'Well, two or three have mentioned it to me, but I have never encouraged them to start a campaign.' Then he said, 'You know, you'll get it. You're young. Dr. Wallace Bassett is one of the greatest leaders we have ever had, and he is not appreciated. I'd like to plead with you to call off your dogs, your hounds, this time and step aside for Dr. Bassett and let him be elected.' I said, 'Well, I don't take a second place to any man in admiration for Dr.

Bassett and all that, and I would consider calling off the hounds if I had put out any. God is my witness, I have not promoted this thing'."

J. D. suspected that Job's friends were at work. Dr. Robert G. Lee told him afterwards, "You know, beloved, several people, who make up a self-appointed committee, came to me and told me that you would ruin the image of Southern Baptists if you were elected president. They said, 'Did you know he smokes?' I said, 'Yes, unfortunately, I know he smokes.' They countered, 'Did you know he tells off-color jokes?' I laughed and went on, 'Beloved, I have heard Dr. Grey tell some funny stories, but I have never heard him tell one I would call a dirty story.' They recalled a story you later told to my Brotherhood."

The Grey fox had gone up to Memphis to address three hundred men in the Bellevue Brotherhood and opened with, "Well, brethren, I had thought tonight I would speak to you on a nice little peppy topic, 'Pay Day Some Day,' but I have decided against it. Dr. Lee and I, both being ex-presidents of the Southern Baptist Convention, are somewhat like the boy who was a page to the Pope at the Vatican. His job every morning was to go in and say, 'Your Holiness, it's eight in the morning; the sun is shining and the people are all happy.' The Pope would reply, 'Thank you, son. God and I know it. God and I know everything.' That went on morning after morning, and the kid got tired of the monotony; so one day he decided to vary it. He went in and, as usual, said, 'Your Holiness, it's eight in the morning, the sun is shining and the people are all happy.' The Pope replied his usual, 'Thank you, son. God and I know. God and I know everything.' 'Huh,' the page answered, 'you're nutty as a fruit cake. It's four o'clock in the afternoon, it's raining like hell, and a revolution is on.'

When I told that story the men roared. Dr. Lee, who was sitting there, turned red and chuckled and then he started laughing. Dr. Lee turned to the Job's friends' committee and said, 'Well, brethren, he told that story to my Brotherhood, and I thought it was a funny story. If I had been telling it, I'd have left the word hell out'."

Another well-meaning brother cornered Kearnie Keegan to ask his assistance in stopping the runaway Grey. "Kearnie, you have more influence on J. D. than anybody else that I know of. I was for J. D. until I got out here, but I am staying at the Sir Francis Drake Hotel, and according to the boys in the lobby, Grey will be cut to mincemeat if he is nominated. He won't even get a look-in. I think you ought to tell J. D. to withdraw his name." Kearnie's reply was: "If you want him told, you tell him. I don't tell him anything; I don't think anybody else can. And, furthermore, I don't know that you have the correct consensus on this matter."

J. D.'s attitude toward the presidency was like that of C. C. Warren, a former president, who said, "I have never tried to run for any office; and if the brethren elect me now because they know me and because they appreciate me, it's because I have always tried to do every job Baptists assigned me to do to the best of my ability, whether it's to be the obituary chairman of my association, or missions chairman, or whatever. I have tried to serve my denomination."

The Grey Sage agrees with all of this and adds, "Of all the men I know, no man is more entitled to say that and to tell the truth than C. C. Warren, because according to my viewpoint, he is a great and wonderful man. He represents a vanishing breed."

J. D.'s attitude toward the critics of his style in and out of the presidential podium is stated succinctly, "In what humility I possess, let me agree that I am misunderstood many times. I have never worried, though, about being mis-understood. Somebody once said, 'Explanations are not nec-essary. Your enemies won't believe it and your friends don't need it.' Pope John XXIII expressed it beautifully in a letter to a friend: 'If you hear anything good about me, praise the Lord as I do, for He has done it all. If you hear criticisms, pray for me if the criticism is just; and, if it is unjust, forgive whoever utters it'."

## In the Arena

Dr. J. D. Grey was nominated for the presidency by Dr. John Jeter Hurt, President of Union University, Grey's alma mater. The Late Dr. Hurt had nominated more men for presi-dent who were eventually elected than any other man in the history of the Southern Baptist Convention. J. D. had not known until he arrived in San Francisco that Hurt would place his name before the messengers.

In Hurt's book, *This Is My Story*, he recalls the moment: "I wanted him when we met in San Francisco, 1951, because I had been his pastor in Jackson; I was president of Union University, at which he graduated, and he would be the youngest president we ever had. Conventionally, he was born in Kentucky, educated in Tennessee and Texas, had proven his leadership by building up the First Baptist of New Or-leans against heavy odds, and was regarded as a pulpiteer all the way from Temple Baptist in Los Angeles to Tremont Temple in Boston, both of which had coveted his services. Not only so, he knew how to dive deep when proper, and how to trumpet the evangelistic note on all occasions. Be-sides, as president he would look the part, speak the part, act the part. I told the people all this; they agreed with me, and were not disappointed."

President Grey surpassed the confidence of his friends. He

proved to be one of the most versatile and accomplished presidents in the history of the Southern Baptist Convention or any other religious body. As a presiding officer he demonstrated a grasp of parliamentary procedure compared to the classical masters in this field. In the heat of an open floor debate he was fair to all sides. His presidential addresses were superbly crafted and unveiled as thoughtful, relevant, optimistic, and biblical declarations of faith. He exhibited great personal charm.

When Hurt was nominating the next president, J. W. Storer, in 1953, he pointed to the opposition surrounding one of the men under consideration because of his position as a denomination executive. No names were mentioned, but the context made the reference plain.

Grey, presiding, interrupted: "Sir, are you speaking against someone or nominating?"

Hurt: "Is not a man allowed to build his own fences?"

With that, Grey bowed from the waist in an apologetic gesture. The convention roared and Storer was elected.

Some observers believe that Storer, who had been defeated previously when Grey was elected, got the votes at this time because of the humor thus injected. The crowd, not knowing of the friendship between Grey and Hurt, assumed that one from the floor had triumphed over the president.

Unlike Job's friends, various ones commented to him, personally and editorially, words of praise. Concerning his nomination and presidency, President Grey recalls a visit with the late Walter Pope Binns, then president of Williams Jewell College: "After delivering an address at Missouri Baptist Convention in the fall of 1951, Binns suggested: 'J. D., let's go to my room, smoke a cigar, and shoot the bull.' Instead we went to my room. Binns took a comfortable chair and said: 'You know (as he unwrapped a cigar that I had given him and lit it) that address tonight was the utterance of a real statesman. You have been the most misunderstood man that has ever served as president of the Convention or attained any place of leadership. Many of the brethren said when you were elected that you would just be a buffoon—always wise-cracking and cutting up—that you would probably embarrass us throughout the year. By the way, they are changing their tune now.' I told him then, 'Well, I never had out my agents to try to interpret me. I go along as I am and people find me out. If they don't, well, I guess they won't."

During the Miami Convention Ted Adams stopped Grey at the Columbus Hotel and said, "J.D., I never doubted a minute that you would be an excellent nominee. Although I have known and appreciated you for what you were, some of the brethren had misgivings that you would be too one-sided in your attitudes and your rulings. It is an accepted fact now that you are fair in all your statements."

### Postscript

The interest in the election ran high. Several couples, going out to dinner, got back to the convention center well past the time for the session to begin. The results of the election were to have been announced. Mistaking the crowd streaming from the Music Hall as messengers to the convention, one of the party rolled down the car window and inquired of a stroller, "Who was elected president?" The confused San Franciscan answered, "Damned if I know; I guess it was Truman!" He had spoken the truth unknowingly. J. D. Grey was indeed the True Man elected and needed as president of the Southern Baptist Convention, the greatest honor his fellow Baptists could accord. When the temperature of the gatherings rose in disagreement, True Man remembered and repeated the sage advice from Truman: "If you can't stand the heat, stay out of the kitchen."

> Yours is the Earth and everything that's in it,
> And—which is more—you'll be a Man, my son!

Rudyard Kipling

# INTRODUCING THE SAINT

*Pastor,* First Baptist Church, New Orleans, 1937–
   Membership, 1937: 1,536; 1969: 4,000.
    Budget, 1937: $26,000.00; 1969: $518,000.00.
   Church Property, $3,000,000.00.
   First Baptist Church, Denton, Texas, 1934–1937.
   Tabernacle Baptist Church, Ennis, Texas, 1931–1934.
   Vickery Baptist Church, Dallas, Texas, 1929–1931.
   Student Pastorates, Tennessee, 1925–1929.

*Birthplace,* Princeton, Kentucky, December 18, 1906,
   Paducah, Kentucky 1914–1925.

*Family,* Married Lillian Tooke, 1927
   Twin daughters,, born 1941, Mrs. Martha Ann
   Cantrell, New Orleans; Mrs. Mary Beth Burg, New
   Orleans
   Grandchildren, Bryant Curtis Cantrell, Patrick Grey
   Cantrell, Joe David Burg

*Education,* Tilghman High School, Paducah, Diploma, 1925,
   Union University, A.B., 1929, Southwestern Baptist
   Theological Seminary, Th.M., 1932.

*Honorary Degrees,* D.D., Union University, 1938.
   LL.D., Louisiana College, 1952.
   D.D., Baylor University, 1953.

*Ordained,* Immanuel Baptist Church, Paducah, Kentucky,
   1925.

*Church and Denomination Offices,*
   Pastor.
   President, Southern Baptist Convention, 1951–1953
   (Youngest elected President at the time).

President, Louisiana Baptist Convention, 1949–1950.

Moderator, New Orleans Baptist Association, 1943–1944.

Baptist Hour (SBC) Speaker, 1949.

Executive Committee Member, Baptist World Alliance, 1950–

At various times members of Agency and Institution Boards of Southern Baptist Convention, Louisiana Baptist Convention, New Orleans Baptist Association, Baptist General Convention of Texas. Currently member of Board of Trustees, Southern Baptist Hospital; Board of Trustees, Louisiana College.

*Church Related Offices,*

Chairman, Billy Graham New Orleans Crusade, 1954.

President, New Orleans Federation of Churches, 1957.

President, Louisiana Moral and Civic Foundation, 1956.

Mission Preacher, U.S. Air Force, 1959.

Currently Cabinet Member, Greater New Orleans Federation of Churches; Board Member, New Orleans Baptist Seaman's Service; Chaplain, Navy League of New Orleans.

*Civic Action,*

Board Member, New Orleans Chapter Boy Scouts of America.

New Orleans Chapter, American Red Cross.

United Fund.

Metropolitan Area Committee.

National Aeronautics and Space Administrative Co-
ordinating Committee, New Orleans.

President, Metropolitan Crime Commission of New
Orleans.

Member, Council for a Better Louisiana (CABLE).

Treasurer, Information Council of the American
(INCA).

Honorary Member, Association for Retarded Children, New Orleans.

Life Member, Salvation Army Advisory Board of
New Orleans Metropolitan Area.

Member, New Orleans Council on Naval Affairs.

Board Member, Stanton Manor, Inc., New Orleans.

Member, Committee on 250th Anniversary of the
Founding of New Orleans.

Member, Louisiana Commission on Law Enforcement
and Administration of Criminal Justice and its
Executive Committee.

Member, Director, Citizens for Support of Public
Schools.

*Fraternal,*

Kiwanis Club of New Orleans, member over 30 years
Alpha Tau Omega.

*Who's Who,*

Listed in "Who's Who in America" and   in "Who's
Who in the South and Southwest."

*Awards and Honors,*

"Unselfish Service" Award, Union University, 1952.
"Honorary Citizen of Oklahoma" awarded by Governor Raymond Gary, 1956.

**161**

"Valuable Citizen" certificate awarded by two mayors of New Orleans.

"In Appreciation" plaque presented by City Council of New Orleans, 1962.

Silver Medallion awarded for service to United Fund, 1969.

"Honorary Citizen" of Dallas, awarded, 1965.

Honorary Citizen in over twelve other cities.

Honorary Deputy Sheriff in ten counties of four states.

"Duke of Paducah" distinction, awarded by Paducah mayor, 1959.

"Kentucky Colonel," "Tennessee Colonel," "Louisiana Colonel," awarded by respective governors.

"Meritorious Service" plaque awarded by New Orleans Federation of Churches, 1962.

"Distinguished Service Award" given by Louisiana Moral and Civic Foundation, 1956.

"Certificate of Appreciation" given by Louisiana Baptist Convention, 1962.

"Legion of Honor" certificate awarded by Kiwanis International.

Honorary membership in Waffenschule 50 presented by U.S. Air Force, Erding Air Base, Germany, 1959.

*Speaker,*

Church groups and assemblies through U.S. and world including military bases; college, civic, community gatherings; Chamber of Commerce Meetings; professional and business conventions; International Kiwanis Convention, convocations, commencement and baccalaureate occasions; Community Chest and United Fund Kick-off rallies; Evangelistic rallies and crusades including London Billy Graham Crusade; Regular Sunday Radio and TV Gospel preacher; Inaugurated Prayer for Peace preceding Sugar Bowl Game in New Orleans.

# NOTES

Vignette 2

1 Kenneth S. Wuest, *The Gospels: An Expanded Translation* (Grand Rapids: William B. Eerdmans Publishing Co., 1956), p. 98.
2 Samuel H. Miller, *Man The Believer* (Nashville: Abingdon Press, 1968), pp. 43, 44.
3 Miller, *Op. cit.*, p. 13.

Vignette 3

1 *Learning Through Controversy* (Philadelphia: The United Presbyterian Church in the U.S.A., 1961), p. 8.
2 Louis A. Safian, *Two Thousand Insults* (New York: Pocket Books Div. Simon & Schuster, Inc., 1966), p. 9 in Introduction.

Vignette 4

1 Robert A. Raines, *Secular Congregation* (New York: Harper & Row, Publishers, 1968), p. 20.
2 James S. Stewart, *Heralds of God* (New York: Scribner, 1946), Preface.
3 J. B. Phillips, *Ring of Truth* (New York: Macmillan Co., 1967), Foreword.
4 J. B. Phillips, *Make Men Whole* (New York: Macmillan Co., 1945), p. 44.
5 Robert Frost, *Chief Modern Poets of England & America* (New York: The Macmillan Co., 1943), p. 573.
6 Carlyle Marney, *These Things Remain* (New York—Nashville: Abingdon—Cokesbury Press, 1953), pp. 101, 102.
7 Morris Bishop, *The Perforated Spirit* (New York: *The New Yorker Magazine Inc.*, 1955).
8 David Poling, *The Last Years of the Church* (Garden City: Doubleday Publishers, 1969), p. 108.
9 C. R. Daley, Editor: *Western Recorder* (Ky.) 1963, Editorial.

Vignette 5

1 Frost, *Op. cit*, p. 584.

Vignette 6

1 Harold E. Kohn, *A Touch of Greatness* (Grand Rapids: William B. Eerdmans Publishing Co., 1965), p. 197.

Vignette 7

1 Roger L. Shinn, *The Tangled World* (New York: Charles Scribner's Sons, 1965), p. 102.
2 Wayne E. Oates, *"Honesty in the Church"* (Wash. D.C.: Baptist Joint Comm. on Public Affairs, April, 1968), p. 1.

3 Foy Valentine, *Citizenship For Christians* (Nashville: Broadman Press, 1965), p. 7.

4 Daniel R. Grant, *The Christian and Politics* (Nashville: Broadman Press, 1968), p. 127.

5 Grant, *Op. cit.*, p. 122.

6 William M. Pinson, Jr. *How To Deal with Controversial Issues* (Nashville: Broadman Press, 1966), p. 39.

7 Roger L. Shinn, Edited by Wayne H. Cowan, *Witness To a Generation* (New York: The Bobbs-Merrill Co., Inc., 1966), p. 67. Reprinted by permission of the publishers.

8 Dr. Percy Hayward, *"Meditation Beside a Ballot Box"* (Great Neck: Pulpit Digest Pub. Co., June 1957), p. 34.

VIGNETTE 8

1 Albert McClellan, The New Times (Nashville: Broadman Press, 1968), p. 78.

VIGNETTE 10

1 Porter Routh, *Meet The Presidents* (Nashville: Broadman Press, 1953), p. 98.